England

England

Jean F. Blashfield

Enchantment of the World
Second Series

Children's Press®

A Division of Grolier Publishing

New York   London   Hong Kong   Sydney
Danbury, Connecticut

Consultant: Karen De Bres, Ph.D., Associate Professor of Geography,
Kansas State University

Please note: *All statistics are as up-to-date as possible at the time of publication.*

Library of Congress Cataloging-in-Publication Data

Blashfield, Jean F.
England / by Jean F. Blashfield.
p. cm. — (Enchantment of the world. Second series)
Includes bibliographical references and index.

Summary: Describes the geography, history, economy, language, religions,
culture, people, plants, and animals of England.
ISBN 0-516-20471-8
1. England—Juvenile literature. [1. England.] I. Title. II. Series.
DA27.5.B58 1997
942—dc21   97-5662
                                                                          CIP
                                                                           AC

This book is dedicated to
Frances Bradbrooke Funnell
flatmate extraordinaire.
Thanks for introducing me to
all that is good in England.

Cover photo:
A guard outside
Buckingham Palace

A trail in Derbyshire

Contents

CHAPTER

 ONE   This Realm, This England......................... 8

TWO   The Fortress Built by Nature..................... 14

THREE   Nature for People................................. 27

FOUR   The Making of England.......................... 33

FIVE   Of Kings, Queens, and Parliaments............. 54

SIX   The Business of Business 72

SEVEN   The English People............................... 88

EIGHT   Popes and Parishes............................... 96

NINE   Shakespeare, the Beatles, and Football Players.. 105

TEN   The Ingredients of Daily Life.................... 118

Stonehenge on the Salisbury Plain

Timeline **128**

Fast Facts **130**

To Find Out More **134**

Index **137**

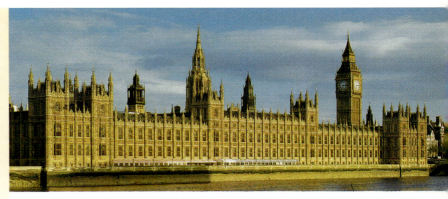

The Houses of Parliament overlook the River Thames.

This Realm, This England

Inch by inch, year by year, thousands of workers moved the massive stones that other workers had chipped out of the earth and shaped into huge slabs. They made roads of rounded logs on which they pushed and pulled the giant stones to their destination on the wide plain. More workers stood the stones on end in the deep pits prepared for them. The standing stones eventually formed circles with horizontal stones resting on top of them.

MANY CENTURIES HAVE PASSED SINCE THE PEOPLE BUILT
the 100-foot (30.5-m) ring of giant building blocks. Just
what their purpose was, we don't know. It probably had
something to do with their religion. It might have been an
observatory that helped them understand the movement of
the puzzling lights we call the stars, Sun, and Moon. Every
June 21, Midsummer Day, the sun rises exactly over a smaller
stone set outside the circles.

This amazing structure is called Stonehenge. It was built as
long as 2,000 years before anyone settled in the place 80 miles
(129 km) away that would become London.

Who were these people and why did they spend so much
effort in building Stonehenge and other stone circles? For a
long time, people thought Stonehenge was built by priests
called *druids*, but the druids actually came along centuries after
the marvelous structure was built.

Near Stonehenge, archaeologists have found axes like
those used in ancient Greece. Perhaps the intrepid sailors of
Greece sailed beyond the horizon and found a new land.
Today, hundreds of thousands of people journey to England's
Salisbury Plain every year to see Stonehenge, one of the mar-
vels of human history.

Stonehenge is not alone in being one of England's marvels. This small island country was the center of one of the mightiest nations on earth. Its political system has been copied by nations worldwide. Its language has become the most widely spoken across the earth. Its industry became the envy of the world. Its thinkers revolutionized science. Its literature is required reading for people everywhere.

And what is Britain? Great Britain? The British Isles? The United Kingdom? These names are often used interchangeably, but they actually mean different things.

The British Isles are a group of islands that include the big island of Great Britain, the smaller island of Ireland, and still smaller islands strewn around the coasts. England shares the southern portion of Great Britain with Wales and the northern portion with Scotland.

The United Kingdom is a modern nation consisting of the once-separate nations of England, Wales, and Scotland, located on Great Britain. It also includes part of Ireland called Northern Ireland.

The term "Britain" is short for England, Great Britain, or the United Kingdom. A "Briton" is an inhabitant of the island, especially in prehistory.

The term "English," however, cannot be used for all the residents of the British Isles. The people who come from the northern part of Great Britain—Scotland—are Scots. Those from the western bulge of the island—Wales—are Welsh. Even the people who lived in England long ago weren't called English. The term is generally used only for the people who lived on the island after the Roman Empire abandoned it. Then the tribes of Angles, Saxons, and Jutes from northern Europe mingled, and these people came to be called by the single name *Anglish*. The name *England*, then, came from "Angle-land."

ENGLAND

0   150 miles

0   200 kilometers

ATLANTIC OCEAN

North Sea

0° Prime Meridian

SCOTLAND

Glasgow
Edinburgh

UNITED

Newcastle upon Tyne

NORTHERN IRELAND

Solway Firth

Belfast

Isle of Man

KINGDOM

Morecambe Bay

Bradford
Humber

IRELAND

Liverpool
Leeds
Manchester

Dublin

Irish Sea

Mersey
Sheffield

The Wash

ENGLAND

Cork

WALES

Birmingham

St. George's Channel

Cardiff

Severn

London

Bristol Channel

Bristol
Bath

Thames

Dover

Plymouth

Portsmouth
Brighton

Strait of Dover

Land's End

Isle of Wight

English Channel

Isles of Scilly

Lizard Point

Channel Islands

FRANCE

Geopolitical map of England

An Island that Spans the World

Because England has 1,150 miles (1,851 km) of seacoast and no place on the island is more than 75 miles (121 km) from water, the sea plays a major role in English life and history. For centuries, it was regarded as dangerous because enemies could sail across it to invade. But when the people united, they turned their island into a fortress, and the sea became the moat around their green castle. Later, the sea became the path that Englishmen used to sail away and build the wealthiest nation on Earth.

The past surrounds the people of England. Their history is known worldwide because so much of it is also the world's history. But the English don't live in the past. In fact, some people think that the English create the future.

The rocky shore of Northumberland is only a small part of England's coastline. The sea has always played an important role in England's history and culture.

The Fortress Built by Nature

Great Britain was not an island until about 8,000 years ago. It had been attached to the mainland of Europe by hills of chalk. Then, with the melting of the great ice sheets that covered Europe during the last Ice Age, the rising ocean tides ate at the chalk. They crushed it and carried it away until water flooded the low-lying area between England and France. Britain became an island fortress.

ENGLAND IS A COMPACT REGION WITH MANY DIFFERENT kinds of scenery. It makes up about 54 percent of the United Kingdom. In that small area, it has mountains, valleys, marshland, moors, big lakes, plains, and cliffs. It is divided into forty-six counties, distributed among eight regions: South East, South West, East Anglia, East Midlands, West Midlands, Yorkshire and Humberside, North, and North West.

England's border with Scotland lies along the River Tweed and the Cheviot Hills, then meanders southwest to the Solway Firth. (A *firth* is a Scottish version of a *fjord*—an arm of the sea that extends inland, often between cliffs.) The border with Wales runs southward in a wavy line from

Geographical Features

Area: 50,356 square miles (130,422 sq km)—more than half the United Kingdom as a whole, and a little larger than the state of Louisiana

Highest Elevation: Scafell Pike in the Lake District, 3,210 feet (978 m)

Lowest Elevation: usually sea level, but when the tide is out near Ely in the Fen Country, a small section of exposed land is actually several feet below sea level

Longest River Strictly in England: the Thames, 215 miles (346 km) long (The Severn, which rises in Wales, is 5 miles (8 km) longer.)

Largest Lake: Windermere in the Lake District, 10 miles (16 km) long

Largest City: London

Counties

1 Avon	17 Greater London	33 Nottinghamshire
2 Bedfordshire	18 Greater Manchester	34 Oxfordshire
3 Berkshire	19 Hampshire	35 Shropshire
4 Buckinghamshire	20 Hereford & Worcester	36 Somerset
5 Cambridgeshire	21 Hertfordshire	37 South Yorkshire
6 Cheshire	22 Humberside	38 Staffordshire
7 Cleveland	23 Isle of Wight	39 Suffolk
8 Cornwall	24 Kent	40 Surrey
9 Cumbria	25 Lancashire	41 Tyne & Wear
10 Derbyshire	26 Leicestershire	42 Warwickshire
11 Devon	27 Lincolnshire	43 West Midlands
12 Dorset	28 Merseyside	44 West Sussex
13 Durham	29 Norfolk	45 West Yorkshire
14 East Sussex	30 North Yorkshire	46 Wiltshire
15 Essex	31 Northhamptonshire	
16 Gloucestershire	32 Northumberland	

the mouth of the River Dee to the mouth of the Wye River on the Severn Estuary. The wavy line follows a ridge of land, or *dyke*, built 1,200 years ago by Offa, a powerful Anglo-Saxon king. He wanted to keep the people who inhabited Wales out of his kingdom of Mercia.

The remainder of England's border is its coastline on the North Sea, the English Channel, and the Irish Sea. The coastline is about 1,150 miles (1,851 km) long. England is closest to France—only 22 miles (35.4 km)—at the Strait of Dover.

The Shape of the Land

For the most part, the island of Great Britain is divided into highland and lowland regions. The highlands are located mostly in Scotland, but they extend into England primarily in the Pennine Mountains, often called the "spine" or "backbone" of England. They curve down into central England, ending just south of Manchester. The valleys in the Pennines are called *dales*. East of Wales and south of the Pennines, the region called the Midlands is fairly low and slopes toward the southeast.

The major indentations in the coast of England are the estuaries of large rivers. Estuaries are sunken river mouths up which the salty water of the sea can flow, mixing freshwater and salt water. They are great places for wildlife as well as harbors for boats. The Humber, Mersey, and Thames are the largest rivers with major estuaries.

The Humber, on the northeast coast, is joined by the Trent and several smaller rivers. It served as a highway into the heart of England for Viking invaders. It is surrounded by *wolds*, which are open, hilly areas, mostly without trees.

South of the wolds lies a large, almost rectangular bay called the Wash. It is surrounded by the Great Fens, which are

The rolling countryside of southwest England

Opposite: **Map of England's counties**

The Fortress Built by Nature   **17**

grassy wetlands. Fens, like bogs, are spongy to walk on because ancient vegetation has piled up and holds water. Like the Dutch across the North Sea, the fen residents worked for many centuries to drain the land. During the 1600s, a Dutch engineer drained the English fens. Almost 500,000 acres (200,000 ha) of good farmland was the result.

The bulge of land south of the Wash to the Thames Estuary is called the Broads of Norfolk, Suffolk, and Essex. The Broads are flat marshes cut by narrow lakes and streams that can be navigated by boat. Today, the Broads are a popular tourist attraction.

The mouth of the Thames was, for several centuries, one of the busiest estuaries in the world. Ships by the thousands left the London docks, carrying goods to world nations and returning with raw materials for British factories. Like most of eastern England, the area around the Thames Estuary is low and flat.

The southernmost part of England is a peninsula called the West Country. It is made up of the counties of Somerset, Devon, and Cornwall. Lizard Point, off the tip of Cornwall, is the southernmost point of the English mainland. The westernmost

Topographical map of England

point is Land's End, a short distance along the coast from Lizard Point, but 3,290 miles (5,295 km) straight across uninterrupted ocean from North America.

Bristol Channel lies between the West Country and Wales. This huge bay leads to the estuary of the Severn River. Just north of the Welsh border on the River Dee is the estuary of the Mersey River. The city of Liverpool stands on this estuary. The big industrial city of Manchester is connected to the Mersey by the Manchester Ship Canal. Still farther north is Morecambe Bay, where the spectacular Lake District begins. England's highest peak and largest lake are both in the Lake District.

Downs and Moors

Much of southern England consists of low chalk hills called the Downs. Downs are grassy, usually treeless uplands made of chalk—a type of soft limestone. (The chalk used in playing hop-

A woman hikes by Blea Water in the Lake District. Lake District National Park is England's largest national park.

The white cliffs of Dover

scotch or writing on blackboards is made in a factory, not found in nature.)

In the middle of the Berkshire Downs, Hampshire Downs, and Marlborough Downs is Salisbury Plain, best known as the location of Stonehenge. Southeast of London is a region called the North Downs, which stretch to the Strait of Dover. The chalk in this region is so light in color that the cliffs here have become famous as the "white cliffs of Dover." The cliffs sometimes are undermined by the sea and break off.

Moors are treeless upland areas, too, but they are generally covered with a layer of peat that holds water. Low-growing evergreen plants called heather grow on the moors, giving a moor the alternate name of *heath*. There are three main moors in southern England—Dartmoor in Devon, Exmoor on the Devon and Somerset border, and Bodmin Moor in Cornwall. These moors often seem desolate because fierce winds from the Atlantic Ocean whip across them with no trees to soften the blast. There is also moorland in North Yorkshire.

Rivers and Lakes

The River Thames (pronounced *tehms*) rises in the Cotswold Hills and flows eastward across southern England. For hundreds of years, the Thames was the main highway to London. From 1450 to 1850, the region had weather that was colder than normal. During this "Little Ice Age," the Thames often froze in winter, and Frost Fairs were held on the ice. The last time such a fair was held on the Thames was in 1814. After that, the river was made deeper so that the tide could flow farther upriver. The Thames no longer froze.

At Greenwich on the Thames, King Charles II built the Royal Observatory. Centuries later, an international agreement set an invisible line running through Greenwich as the 0° line of longitude from which all distances on the earth's surface are measured.

The Thames and other rivers in industrial parts of England were once so polluted that no edible fish could live in them. Then, in the 1960s, a cleanup campaign began, and gradually the fish came back.

The Horse on the Hill

In Wiltshire, near the source of the Thames, there is a low hill on which ancient people carved the figure of a giant horse 374 feet (114 m) long. No one knows for sure when the horse was carved through the topsoil into the chalk beneath. It may have been done by the Saxons only ten centuries ago, or it may stem from Iron Age Celts who lived there 2,300 years ago.

Most of England's lakes are found in the Lake District in the Cumbrian Mountains in the North. Lake Windermere, at more than 10 miles (16 km) long, is the largest lake in England. Scafell Pike is the nation's highest peak.

England Offshore

A group of islands is located in the English Channel, much closer to France than to England. The four main Channel Islands are Jersey, Guernsey, Alderney, and Sark. They seem like part of the United Kingdom and recognize Queen Elizabeth as their sovereign, but they are, in fact, separate entities. So, too, is the Isle of Man, located in the Irish Sea. Both places have their own legislature and laws. The Isle of Man's legislature is perhaps the world's oldest. The United Kingdom takes care of these islands' international relations and defense.

Other islands near Great Britain are part of England. The Isle of Wight off the southern coast is separated from the mainland by a strait called the Solent. Ships coming into port at Southampton have to go around the island, which was Queen Victoria's favorite vacation spot.

The Isles of Scilly (a name the residents prefer to the "Scilly Isles," which sounds too much like "silly") consist of about 100 small islands plus numerous rocks. They lie 25 to 36 miles (40 to 58 km) off the coast of Land's End in Cornwall. Only five of the islands are inhabited year-round. The largest is St. Mary's, where most of the people live. These islands sit in the Gulf Stream and have a much warmer climate than most of England. The warm waters of the Gulf Stream allow the islands to grow flowers in the middle of winter when parts of Britain may be snow covered. Palm trees also flourish there.

"Looks Like Rain"

It is often said that the first thing two English people talk about on meeting is the weather. Indeed, the weather is amazingly variable over such a small area, and its rapid changes can always provide a subject for conversation.

England is on the same latitude as Newfoundland, Canada. But unlike Newfoundland's cold weather, England's climate is graced by the Gulf Stream. This big ocean current carries warm water from the Caribbean Sea, letting flowers bloom in February and palm trees grow in southern England, especially along the area referred to as the Cornish Riviera. The combination of moisture and warmth keeps England green throughout the year. It also keeps England from getting too warm in summer when the Gulf Stream is cooler than the land.

The coastal areas are the warmest, with an average winter temperature above 40°F (4°C). Only the South East is likely to average much above 60°F (16°C) in July and August. Anything above 75°F (24°C) is considered a heat wave.

It does not rain as much in England as its reputation holds. The air currents coming across the ocean bring rain to England fairly evenly throughout the year, so that an average month may have a little rain on about half the days. But the rain rarely amounts to much—at least in the South East. The air currents don't spread the rain evenly throughout the country. The Lake District averages 30 inches (330 cm) of rain each year, but may get up to 200 inches (508 cm), while London gets only 20 inches (50.8 cm)—about the same as South Dakota. Snow falls in the London area only four or five times each winter and rarely stays long on the ground.

In general, England's climate is similar to the Pacific Coast areas of Oregon and Washington states, which have the same

Looking at English Cities

Birmingham, a city in the county of West Midlands, has a population of about one million. The city probably got its name from the de Bermingham family, lords of the manor of Birmingham from 1150 to 1166. One of England's largest industrial centers, the city has a large output of steel and many highly skilled engineers, which make it an

ideal spot for the British auto industry. But long before the auto industry arrived, Birmingham was famous for armaments, jewelry, and other crafts.

Leeds (above), located in the county of West Yorkshire, stands on the Aire River and has a population of about 724,400. Leeds was founded in the eighteenth century, though there was a fort at the same spot in Roman times. The city is largely the creation of England's Industrial Revolution and produces textiles, furniture, paper, leather, and electrical equipment.

Sheffield, England's fourth-largest city, has a population of 530,100. It is located on the Don River in the county of South Yorkshire. Chaucer referred to a "Sheffield thwitel," the ancestor of the modern pocketknife, in *The Canterbury Tales*. Sheffield has been famous for its knives and other cutting tools since the Middle Ages.

Liverpool (below), located on the Mersey Estuary, has a population of 474,000. It boasts one of the largest harbors in the world and is a center of transatlantic shipping as well as a major manufacturing city. Liverpool was founded in 1173 by Henry II. The city's name is connected with the mythological Liver Bird, a seagull or cormorant-like bird displayed on the city's coat of arms.

Manchester has a population of 431,100. The city sprang from the Roman settlement of Mancunium—hence the name "Manchester"—and played an important part in the Industrial Revolution. Much of the city was destroyed by German bombs in World War II, and its textile industry has given way to mechanical engineering and high-technology industries.

moderate, cloudy weather. However, England can also get weather that has formed over Europe and Asia. When the wind changes direction and the temperatures are extremely cold or extremely hot, the weather has usually come from the continent.

Devastating Weather

Hurricanes form in the Caribbean, brush past the United States, and then turn seaward into the Atlantic, but they rarely survive long enough to hit Europe. Great Britain has major windstorms, however. On the night of October 15–16, 1987, winds blowing 100 miles per hour (161 kph) hit southern England. These were the highest winds ever recorded in London, and they uprooted millions of trees, including rare old plant specimens at Kew Gardens. Only twenty-seven months later, another storm hit the British Isles and Europe with winds as high as 110 mph (177 kph). Forty-six people died in Britain, and an equal number of deaths were reported on the continent.

London was once famous for its terrible fogs called "pea-soup" fogs because they were thick and greenish, preventing people from seeing anything more than a few feet away. They were also called "killer" fogs because people with lung problems could not breathe. The Sherlock Holmes stories by Arthur Conan Doyle made these fogs famous throughout the world.

It wasn't the fog itself that made these episodes so deadly; it was pollution in the air from the burning coal used for heat and industry. After the use of coal was outlawed in metropolitan areas in 1956, the fogs that could kill disappeared.

Nature for People

England is a crowded country. Fortunately, nature has always been important to its inhabitants. Long ago, cities were given parks. Well before the environmental movement caught on around the world, England made an effort to create "green belts" around the major cities—areas where people could not build.

This path through Derbyshire allows people to travel by horse or on foot.

Pathways across private land are traditionally kept open because people have a historical right to use them. These public rights-of-way allow the English, who are great walkers, to explore vast areas of their country that they might not otherwise see. One walking path more than 600 miles (966 km) long follows the coast around the West Country. If you were a crow, the distance would not be nearly so great, but the rocky coast has many inlets and small bays that are fascinating to explore.

Plans are underway for a national trail for horse and mountain-bike riders. The Pennine Bridleway will take riders 208 miles (335 km) through the Pennine Mountains from Cumbria to Derbyshire.

Only about 7 percent of English land is forested, an amount far below the rest of Europe. Owners of agricultural land are now encouraged to return land to forest in exchange for a small annual payment. This plan increases the amount of forest, which serves both as wildlife habitat and as a source of timber that doesn't have to be imported.

Gardens of England

While many wild areas have gradually given way to agriculture and housing, the English have made up for it by enthusiastically planting gardens. Certain parts of England have been planted for so long that it's hard to tell what is natural. On the island of Tresco, one of the Isles of Scilly, more than 5,000 varieties of plants from all over the world grow in the Abbey Garden. It was started almost 1,000 years ago when the location was a monastery.

Great houses have had well-planned and well-kept gardens for generations. They often employed as many gardeners outdoors as servants indoors. The style was encouraged by an eighteenth-century landscape gardener called Capability Brown (his real name was Lancelot). He designed gardens to look as naturally wild as possible.

The Royal Botanic Gardens at Kew, near London, was founded in 1759 with the object of collecting as many specimen plants as possible from around the world. Kew Gardens is a beautiful place to visit, but its work behind the scenes is more important. The Seed Bank at Kew contains one of the world's largest collection of seeds of wild plants that are rapidly becoming extinct all over the world. It is hoped that if scientists someday discover that an extinct species will be useful in medicine, Kew will have the seeds in its collection.

Although most of England has been turned into farm fields or pasture, for centuries those fields provided shelter for wildlife in an unusual way. Instead of being bordered by fences, many fields were separated by rows of bushes that had grown old and tangled. Called *hedgerows*, they were natural homes for many birds and small mammals. Unfortunately, many old hedgerows have been cut down by farmers in recent years.

English people have long been avid birders. Many people maintain lifetime lists of birds they have seen and identified. The variety of habitats found in England provides homes for many species of birds. Also, almost every month, some birds pass through England on their way to or from somewhere else.

Wild Mammals

Gone are the wolves and the wild boars—they were hunted out of existence long ago. But England still has a good variety of large mammals.

Exmoor and the Lake District have red deer, while the roe deer is found only in the West Country. (Both of these species thrive in the Scottish Highlands.) The fallow deer is found in many areas of England.

Even in the bushes of busy London, the European hedgehog can be found. This little mammal, often compared to the porcupine, looks and feels more like a large pinecone. Although some species of hares are native to England, the country had no rabbits until they were brought from Europe by the Romans. The rabbits took over large parts of the countryside, often feeding on gardens—as Beatrix Potter observed before creating her story *The Tale of Peter Rabbit*. Badgers are also common on agricultural land. The red fox

A hedgehog

Hoofbeats on the Moors

The most surprising hoofed animals in England are wild ponies. Dartmoor, Exmoor, and the New Forest are home to attractive wild ponies that look like small thoroughbreds. Actually, they're not quite wild—their welfare is supervised by naturalists, and they are used to being approached by people. Once a year they are herded together, checked, and counted. Excess young animals are then sold to private citizens.

is found throughout England, even in the suburbs. Its numbers have never been reduced by the English fondness for foxhunting. However, the little dormouse, made famous in Lewis Carroll's *Alice's Adventures in Wonderland*, is threatened with extinction. Otters are common along the riverbanks, and several species of seals are found along the western coasts.

National Parks

England has seven national parks. Unlike national parks in most other countries, the land in England's national parks is generally privately owned. The Parks Authority works with the owners to manage the land carefully, plan which paths and areas can be open to the public, and provide information.

Dormice are threatened with extinction.

Dartmoor National Park takes up about half of Dartmoor, a rocky plateau with jagged piles of granite called *tors*. Yes Tor is more than 2,000 feet (610 m) high. Exmoor, nearby, is gentler, with some spectacular scenery on the Bristol Channel. Lake District National Park, at almost 900 square miles (2,331 sq km), is the largest of England's national parks. The other national parks are Peak District, North York Moors, Yorkshire Dales, and Northumberland.

A tor, or granite pile, in Dartmoor National Park

The Making of England

In 1993, archaeologists found a human shinbone in a quarry at the town of Boxgrove. The tool-using Boxgrove Man stood over 6 feet (1.8 m) tall and was a hunter-gatherer. This discovery showed historians that England's human history began at least 500,000 years ago.

THEN, ABOUT 5,000 YEARS AGO, OTHER HUMANS CROSSED the English Channel from France to England. They were farmers who took advantage of England's climate. They buried their dead in huge burial mounds called *barrows*. They also began to build monumental stone circles called *henges*.

About the time the oldest part of Stonehenge was built, the Beaker people, known only from their decorated pottery

An aerial view of Stonehenge

beakers, or drinking cups, arrived from the continent. They fortified their towns, probably against the barrow-makers. The Beaker people mined tin in Cornwall and traded it on the continent. They put thousands of people to work enlarging Stonehenge.

Starting about 700 B.C., another group of people began to cross the Channel. Called Celts (pronounced *kelts*), they are the ancestors of the Highland Scots, the Irish, and the Welsh. The Celts were farmers who cleared a great deal of land. They had strong chieftains who built forts, but the forts were not strong enough to withstand the Roman legions.

Roman Britannia

England's recorded history begins with the Roman Empire. Julius Caesar, emperor of Rome, first conquered Gaul (France)

Warrior Woman

Some tribes in England submitted easily to the Romans. Others did not. When the Iceni tribe's king died, the Romans grabbed his property and had his queen, Boudicca (also called Boadicea), whipped. Furious, the powerful woman rallied her own soldiers and led them to Londinium (now London), which she burned to the ground. The Romans retaliated by killing many more Iceni men, women, and children. The queen committed suicide rather than submit to the Roman centurions. Today, a huge monument to the Iceni heroine stands on the bank of the Thames beside the Parliament buildings.

and then tried twice to invade and conquer Pretani (the name that turned into *Britannia*). Each time, his troops were beaten back by the people living there. In A.D. 43, another emperor, Claudius, sent troops, and this time they succeeded. The people Julius Caesar had encountered were later called *Picts*, meaning "painted people." Rather than try to conquer the Picts, the Romans built two walls across northern England to keep them in Scotland. The remains of one wall, called Hadrian's Wall, still stand today.

For almost 400 years, Britain was a province of the Roman Empire. People moved from other Roman provinces to England. Soldiers brought their families and settled, or married local women and gradually merged with the Celts. Many camps were established; all the English towns with "cester" or "chester" in their names developed from Roman camps.

Romans lived well, using slave labor at home and in the fields.

Starting about A.D. 400, Rome called its soldiers home, but many of them were sons of families that had lived in Britannia for several generations. They knew nothing about Rome. Rather than go back to an unknown world, they stayed and became British.

Remains from the Vikings and other early cultures have been unearthed in the British Isles.

Anglo-Saxons and Vikings

As the Romans left, invaders from northern Europe streamed across the Channel and the North Sea. The newcomers were primarily from three Germanic tribes—the Saxons, Angles, and Jutes. They gradually took control as far north as the Firth of Forth in Scotland and southwest to Cornwall.

The true England did not start until the various Anglo-Saxon tribes began to speak one language and develop one culture. During the sixth and seventh centuries, the many small kingdoms joined forces, usually by marriage, until only three great kingdoms remained—Northumbria, Mercia, and Wessex. By that time, the kingdoms were mostly Christian. They were on the verge of uniting when new trouble arrived in the shape of the Norsemen, or Vikings.

About 840, the Vikings began to capture land, destroying villages and monasteries in order to steal their wealth. They took possession of most of central England, a region they called the Danelaw.

The first real opposition to Norse invasions came from Alfred, king of the West Saxons, or Wessex, who ruled from 871. He and his successors gradually took back the Danelaw. King Alfred did three things that gave him the name "Alfred the Great." He stopped the Danish invasion, involved his best people in governing, and turned the people's interest from war to culture. Alfred began writing *The Anglo-Saxon Chronicle*, a record of events in England that was continued for several centuries.

The kingdom of England did not truly exist until A.D. 927, when Athelstan, the king of Wessex and Mercia, also became king of parts of Northumbria. Cornwall, which had long fought off the Anglo-Saxons, gave in and became part of Athelstan's unified kingdom in 936.

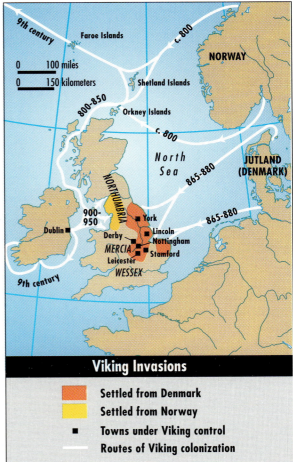

Viking Invasions

■ Settled from Denmark

■ Settled from Norway

■ Towns under Viking control

— Routes of Viking colonization

The last time England was invaded was the year 1066, in an event called the Norman Conquest. The Normans (originally the name meant "Norsemen") were people from a small kingdom called Normandy, now part of France.

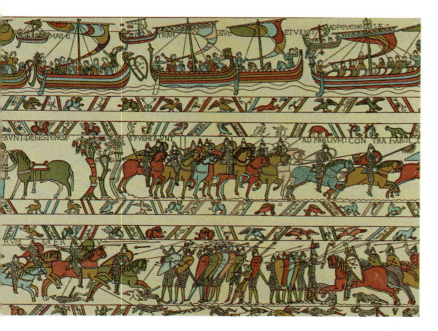

This reproduction of the famous Bayeux Tapestry depicts the Norman invasion of England in 1066.

The English king was Edward the Confessor, who preferred the church to government or families. He left no children to inherit the throne. Harold Godwin, an Anglo-Saxon earl, claimed the throne, but Duke William of Normandy, a distant cousin, decided to fight for possession of England because it was five times larger than Normandy. William and his men invaded England and triumphed over Harold's army at the Battle of Hastings. William the Conqueror was crowned king of England on Christmas Day, 1066.

Saxon lands were confiscated and given to about 180 of William's own knights. Because the knights, called barons, also gave land to their followers, confusion soon reigned about who owned what. William ordered an accounting of land ownership, both to stop the confusion and to make sure he collected all the taxes he was due. What the investigators learned was

A Fort, Castle, Prison, and Tourist Attraction

William the Conqueror built a fort on the north bank of the River Thames inside the remains of the Roman Wall at London. The first building was the central keep, called the White Tower. Begun in 1078, it was built of stone brought to England from Normandy. Over the following centuries, William's fort was enlarged into a castle with new outer walls and additional towers. The whole complex is called the Tower of London. The Tower was both a safe residence for England's monarchs and a prison for traitors. Guards, called yeoman warders and Beefeaters (above), still tend the Tower, wearing the colorful red uniforms that date from the time of Elizabeth I. The Tower of London is the most popular tourist attraction in London.

The Norman Kings

William I	1066–1087
William II	1087–1100
Henry I	1100–1135
Stephen	1135–1154

recorded in *The Domesday Book*. Often called by the fatal-sounding name "Doomsday Book," the name simply means "day of judgment." The book was used to settle disputes.

On August 1, 1086, all the landholders of England came to Sarum Castle at Salisbury and swore allegiance to King William. Only a year after that day, King William died.

One of William's sons, William Rufus, became king of William I's English conquests. After William I was killed in a hunting accident, his youngest son became Henry I, who ruled Normandy and England as one. But when Henry died, the succession—the change from one monarch to the next—was not clear. Stephen, one of Henry's nephews, became the next king, but he and Matilda, Henry's daughter, fought for many years. Stephen made Matilda's son, Henry, his heir, however. Henry II started his rule in 1154, and he and his descendants were given the name Plantagenet.

Henry II appointed his friend Thomas Becket, an Anglo-Saxon, as archbishop of Canterbury. Henry was angered when Becket made decisions based on the idea of the church being superior to the king. The king urged

Richard the Lion-Hearted
fought in the Crusades.

Plantagenet Kings

Henry II	1154–1189
Richard I	1189–1199
John	1199–1216
Henry III	1216–1272
Edward I	1272–1307
Edward II	1307–1327
Edward III	1327–1377
Richard II	1377–1399

someone to get rid of Becket. Four of his knights did so, murdering the archbishop in Canterbury Cathedral. Thomas Becket was declared a saint by the pope, the head of the church in Rome.

Henry's oldest son, Richard, called the Lion-Hearted, spent most of his adult life in the Middle East fighting the Crusades instead of ruling in England. When he died abroad, his brother John became king. John's barons became angry at him for a variety of reasons. On June 15, 1215, they demanded

Opposite: **Henry I**

Lancaster and York Kings

Henry IV	1399–1413
Henry V	1413–1422
Henry VI	1422–1461
Edward IV	1461–1470
Henry VI	1470–1471
Edward IV	1471–1483
Edward V	1483
Richard III	1483–1485

that he meet them in a field at Runnymede on the banks of the Thames near London. They presented him with a document guaranteeing that the king would, like any citizen, submit to law. Rather than chance civil war, John signed the document. In modified form, it became the famed *Magna Carta*, or "the Great Charter." It is regarded as the forerunner of America's Declaration of Independence.

Forming the United Kingdom

Various kings spent decades fighting the local chieftains in Wales. The Plantagenet king Edward I, who succeeded in controlling England's unruly neighbor, declared his son to be Prince of Wales—a title most English monarchs have given their male heirs ever since. About 200 years later, in 1485, Henry Tudor, who came from a Welsh family, became Henry VII of England, and his son, Henry VIII, finally united the two countries.

The Norman barons held most of Ireland in the thirteenth century, but it wasn't until 1541 that the Tudor king Henry VIII forced the Irish to acknowledge him as their king. After he broke with Rome, replacing the Roman Catholic Church in Britain with the Church of England, he also tried to force the Irish to become Protestants. Rebellions, wars, and permanent anger developed over the fact that Catholics had few political rights. In the twentieth century, the southern two-thirds of the island of Ireland broke away from the United Kingdom and became the independent nation called the Republic of Ireland, or Eire.

After the Norman Conquest, the English spent centuries trying to conquer Scotland so that they could control the entire island of Great Britain. Scottish kings frequently enlisted the aid of France to keep them independent. But when the Tudor queen Elizabeth I died in 1603 without an heir, King James VI of Scotland, her cousin, became king of England, too. The United Kingdom had reached the form it has today.

Tudor Kings and Queens

Henry VII	1485–1509
Henry VIII	1509–1547
Edward VI	1547–1553
Lady Jane Grey	1553
Mary I	1553–1558
Elizabeth I	1558–1603

Wars Away and at Home

More than 100 years of on-and-off war with France tested the willingness of the English people to pay taxes for the kings' desires to regain French land. This long period of war began in 1337 when Edward III claimed the French throne on the basis that three French kings had been his uncles. In 1420, English king Henry V was declared heir to French king Charles VI after he married Charles's daughter. But even then, the fighting dragged on for another twenty-four years. Gradually the tide turned against the English, and they gave up their French lands in 1453.

Henry VI was the grandson of Henry IV, duke of Lancaster, whose symbol was a red rose. Lancaster had taken the throne away from Richard II, who was the duke of York. The symbol of the Yorks was a white rose. Those who believed that the Lancasters were the true kings fought those who believed the Yorks should still be the monarchs. The Wars of the Roses went on for more than thirty-five years. They ended in 1485, when Richard III, the last York, was killed on the battlefield

The Wars of the Roses lasted more than thirty-five years.

by Welshman Henry Tudor, a red-rose Lancastrian descended from Edward III. Henry Tudor became Henry VII and married the daughter of York king Edward IV. He thus united the red rose and the white rose and formed a new royal house— the Tudors.

As we'll see in Chapter Eight, the next Tudor king, Henry VIII, broke with the Roman Catholic Church over the issue of divorcing his wife, who had given him a daughter, not a son. When his second wife, Anne Boleyn, produced another daughter, Henry accused her of adultery and had her beheaded. This powerful king then went on to marry four more times. One wife, Jane Seymour, produced a son.

Henry's only son, nine-year-old Edward, became king in 1547. Edward VI was weak from birth and died as a teenager. Henry VIII had changed England forever because he had wanted a son to follow him as king. But the two daughters he didn't want became queens of England.

Building an Empire

In 1497, Tudor king Henry VII sent Italian-born John Cabot and his son, Sebastian, to explore the newly found lands on the other side of the Atlantic Ocean. In the Americas, they came upon great, untouched fishing banks they thought would be perfect for English fishermen. After that, the English sailed the world, out of sheer curiosity as well as the desire to increase their wealth.

Under Elizabeth I (her older half sister, Mary, a Roman Catholic, ruled only long enough to become known as "Bloody Mary" for executing many Protestants), England turned into a seafaring nation. Sir Walter Raleigh tried to colonize the land he called "Virginia" after Elizabeth, the Virgin Queen. Francis Drake became the first Englishman to try to sail around the world. He found treasure by pirating Spanish ships coming from South America. His raids, as well as the Spaniards' staunch belief in the Catholic Church, prompted Spain to send an armada—a great fleet of ships—to invade and capture England.

In 1588, 130 Spanish ships set out for England, but the men aboard had few provisions, and powerful winds

Elizabeth I

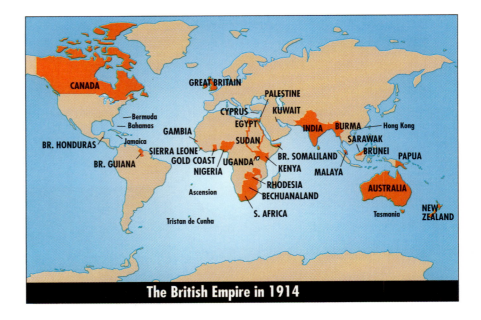

The British Empire in 1914

slowed their passage. They were attacked by the English navy, and a storm blasted them against rocks. A few ships limped back to Spain. After the defeat of the Spanish Armada, English people believed that they were the greatest sailors on earth.

Elizabeth died in 1603 without having married. To find a new monarch, Parliament looked to Scotland, where James Stuart, son of Mary, Queen of Scots and a descendant of Henry VII, was king. He became England's king, too, thus creating the United Kingdom. James's name was given to the new colony established in Virginia, called Jamestown. Later, more colonies were settled in North America, as well as Australia, New Zealand, South Africa, India, various Caribbean islands, and elsewhere. The American Revolution took many colonies out of English hands, but losing them just encouraged Englishmen to look elsewhere. By the mid-1800s, England had built a worldwide empire on which "the sun never set."

Without Parliament, Without King

James I went to London from Scotland with one firm idea—he was king by "divine right" and thus did not have to deal with Parliament. He passed this same attitude onto his son, Charles I. Charles dismissed Parliament and ruled until civil war between Parliament and the king broke out in 1642.

Parliament's army, under Puritan leader Oliver Cromwell of Cambridge, beheaded Charles in 1649. Cromwell, who called himself Lord Protector, then ran the country until his death in 1658. As a Puritan, he believed that the Church of England needed purifying, and he had many castles and churches destroyed. After Cromwell's death, the people demanded that the monarchy be restored, and Charles's son, Charles II, was called to become king.

The Restoration did not end the problems with the monarch, however. The next king, James II, was so pro-Catholic that Parliament brought James II's daughter, Mary, a Protestant, and her

Stuart Rulers	
James I	1603–1625
Charles I	1625–1649
Rule without a monarch	1649–1659
Charles II	1660–1685
James II	1685–1688
William III and Mary II	1689–1694
William III	1694–1702
Anne	1702–1714

Oliver Cromwell in Parliament

George III

husband, Prince William of Orange of the Netherlands, to England as joint rulers. James fled, and William and Mary ruled under strict guidelines that turned England into a constitutional monarchy.

Embroiled in World Events

When Queen Anne, the last of the Protestant Stuarts, failed to produce an heir to the throne, Parliament went to Germany to find a king. James I's daughter had married a monarch from the area called Hanover. One of her descendants was George, elector (or ruler) of Hanover. He became George I, king of England. His grandson, George III, was king when the American colonies rebelled and succeeded in gaining their independence.

The English had little time to relax before being thrown into another war, this time mostly on the continent. For twenty years, England fought a series of wars that came to be called the Napoleonic Wars after the French general Napoleon. Part of the struggle was fought in the United States as the War of 1812. These wars ended in 1815, when Arthur Wellesley, duke of Wellington, beat

Napoleon at the Battle of Waterloo. England then emerged as the most powerful nation on earth.

In 1837, a new queen came to the throne. She was Victoria, who would rule until 1901, giving her name to a long era of great prosperity for the aristocrats and great poverty for the underclasses. Gradually, things changed for the working people. Laws were passed keeping children from hard labor. Trade unions began to organize and to acquire some rights for workers. Schools were established for the nation's children. The lawmakers began to develop a social conscience. But it took two world wars to soften the rigid class structure of the people.

The World at War

Twice in the twentieth century, Germany tried to expand, forcibly taking over neighboring countries. Both times, Britain led the Allied countries in the effort to stop Germany. World War I began for England in 1914, when its soldiers had to go to the continent to help France, even though the German kaiser (like a king) was Queen Victoria's grandson. The war ended in 1918, after the United States sent an army to help. But by that time, 750,000 British soldiers had died. The war had cost so much that England was no longer the mightiest nation on earth.

During the war, the Irish had revolted against the English in the Easter Rebellion of 1916. The English had most of the surviving Irish leaders shot for treason. Immediately after the war, the majority of Irish seats in Parliament were won by

Hanover Rulers and Their Descendants

George I	1714–1727
George II	1727–1760
George III	1760–1820
George IV	1820–1830
William IV	1830–1837
Victoria	1837–1901

House of Saxe-Coburg-Gotha (name taken from Victoria's husband, Albert):

Edward VII	1901–1910
George V	1910–1917

House of Windsor (name taken to eliminate German connection):

George V	1917–1936
Edward VIII	1936
George VI	1936–1952
Elizabeth II	1952–present

Sinn Fein, a political party that believed Ireland belonged only to the 90 percent of the Irish people who were Catholics. Three years of continuous guerrilla warfare on Irish soil finally led to English soldiers withdrawing from Ireland.

Parliament agreed in 1921 to let Ireland be divided. Twenty-six counties formed Eire, or the Irish Republic. The six mostly Protestant counties in the north formed Northern Ireland, which is still part of the United Kingdom. But even today, people in both the Irish Republic and Northern Ireland continue to fight and even bomb England.

Twenty years after World War I ended, Germany once again tried to expand its borders, this time under the brutal Nazi leader, Adolf Hitler. Britain was committed to helping Poland, which was invaded by German troops on September 1, 1939. Hitler was determined to carry the war into England.

After conquering France, the Germans were ready to invade England. For two months in the summer of 1940, British pilots fought German aircraft over the Channel. Day after day, the

During the Blitz of World War II, Londoners took shelter in Underground stations.

pilots took their small fighter planes into the air, trying to prevent the bombers from reaching their targets. Gradually, this "Battle of Britain" paid off. Hitler decided he could not invade.

But bomb England he could. For months, London and nearby towns were bombed in what came to be called the Blitz. Londoners spent long, frightening nights in the Underground (subway) stations to avoid being killed. They emerged each morning to find more of London flattened. St. Paul's Cathedral, designed by Sir Christopher Wren after the Great Fire of London in 1666, became a symbol. As long as it stood each morning, England stood. By a miracle, St. Paul's was never hit.

Soon, almost every nation and colony on Earth was involved in the war. The United States entered in late 1941, when Japan bombed Hawaii. England became the staging area for troops to invade the continent and fight Hitler on his own ground. Huge numbers of troops from the United States, Canada, Australia, and many other nations crossed the Channel from England in June 1944. Within months, the war in Europe was over. Hitler was defeated, and soon Japan was defeated, too.

Even after bombs destroyed much of the city, St. Paul's Cathedral was still standing.

Citizens celebrated in the streets of India when England granted the country independence in 1947.

The End of the Empire

The nation that did so much to free the world from tyranny could no longer afford to support its huge empire. Many of the colonies wanted their freedom. England began releasing its colonies in 1947, when independence was granted to India. Parliament decided to prepare all of Britain's colonies for independence. But it couldn't just leave the colonies on their own right away. It had to make certain that each colony could survive economically and politically without Britain.

Over the next decade, British colonies gained their independence one by one. They became full partners in the Commonwealth of Nations—an organization made up of the United Kingdom and its former colonies. Britain itself began to focus more on its new partners, the European nations of the Common Market, now called the European Union (EU). The sun may have finally set on the British Empire, but a new day has begun for England.

Preserving the Past

England has preserved much of its physical history. At least 2,000 buildings of historic importance—from castles to lock houses on canals, from stately homes to mills—are open to the public. The National Trust owns and operates many of these sites. Others are under the care of English Heritage, which was founded in 1984. These organizations are making sure that England's history remains a lively part of England's future.

The United Nations also has selected a number of places of universal value as World Heritage Sites. They need to be protected and preserved. In England, World Heritage Sites include Canterbury Cathedral, Durham Cathedral and Castle, Studley Royal Gardens and Fountains Abbey, Ironbridge Gorge (the world's first iron bridge), the stone circles at Stonehenge and Avebury, Blenheim Palace, the entire city of Bath, Hadrian's Wall (above), the Tower of London, and the Palace of Westminster.

Of Kings, Queens, and Parliaments

Unlike the United States, the United Kingdom does not have a written constitution. Instead, it has hundreds of years of custom, development, change, and law, which make up what we know as today's government.

54

Queen Elizabeth II and her husband, Prince Philip

The Monarch

AT THE HEART OF THE UNITED Kingdom's government is the monarch—the king or queen. Since 1952, the monarch has been Queen Elizabeth II. Her official title is "Elizabeth the Second, by the Grace of God, of the United Kingdom of Great Britain and Northern Ireland and of Her other Realms and Territories Queen, Head of the Commonwealth, Defender of the Faith."

Westminster Abbey in London has been the site of coronations (crowning ceremonies) since it was built by Edward the Confessor. England's monarch is officially crowned by the archbishop of Canterbury.

The wife of a ruling king is called the queen, and she is also crowned. However, the husband of a ruling queen is not the king. Philip, the duke of Edinburgh and the husband of Queen Elizabeth, is called the prince consort. He was not crowned.

Westminster Abbey

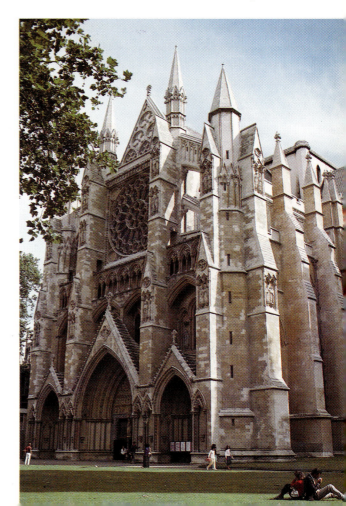

Flags and Dragons

The Union Jack—a flag of red, white, and blue with a red cross through the center—is the official flag of the United Kingdom. England itself has no official flag, but the flag called St. George's Cross has been used for centuries. It consists of the red cross and white background of the Union Jack.

Saint George is the patron saint of England. He was a Roman soldier from about A.D. 300 who was persecuted for turning Christian. Crusaders wore his symbol—the red cross on a white field—into battle. Popular legend says that Saint George slew a dragon, perhaps near the town of Glastonbury, although there is no evidence that he was ever in England—or that England ever had dragons.

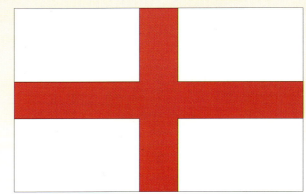

Changes at the Palace

Elizabeth II became queen because her uncle, Edward VIII, abdicated, meaning he gave up the throne. His brother became King George VI. George had no sons, so his elder daughter, Elizabeth, became queen in 1952. Elizabeth's oldest son, Charles, Prince of Wales, is now heir to the throne. Edward VIII abdicated rather than give up the divorced woman he loved, but times change, and the Prince of Wales was divorced from Princess Diana in 1996. Some English people feel that Charles should not become king. Others think that it no longer matters if the king has been divorced.

The Stone of Scone

Since 1296, English monarchs, such as Queen Elizabeth II in 1952 (left), have been crowned while sitting on a plain wooden seat (the Coronation Chair) resting over a large block of sandstone called the Stone of Scone. The stone had been used in the coronations of Scottish kings since 839. The stone was removed from Scotland by Edward I and kept as a symbol that the English ruled the Scots. For 700 years, English possession of the coronation stone angered the Scots. In 1996, the stone was returned to the Scots, who agreed that it can be "borrowed" and taken to Westminster Abbey whenever a new monarch is crowned.

Charles and Diana have two sons. The elder, Prince William of Wales, is next in line of succession.

The queen lives primarily at Buckingham Palace in London, but Windsor Castle has been the official royal residence since the twelfth century. There are a number of other royal palaces, including Sandringham in Norfolk, Hampton Court on the Thames, and Kensington and St. James's in London. Even though royalty has not lived in St. James's Palace since Queen Victoria's time, ambassadors from other countries are said to be going to the "Court of St. James."

Princess Diana with her sons, William and Harry

Over the centuries, some people have complained about taxpayers supporting the splendid monarchy, since monarchs are major landowners and have considerable income from their land. Nothing changed, however, until recent years. The English were disturbed by the divorces and other "nontraditional" happenings going on in the royal family, so many people thought that the financing of the monarchy should change, too.

The queen now pays income taxes for the first time. She even opened up Buckingham Palace to tourists to earn money to pay for rebuilding the part of Windsor Castle destroyed by fire in 1992. The rebuilding is expected to cost close to $90 million, an amount the British will not have to pay in taxes.

"Trooping the Colour," a traditional celebration when the queen reviews her troops, takes place outside Buckingham Palace.

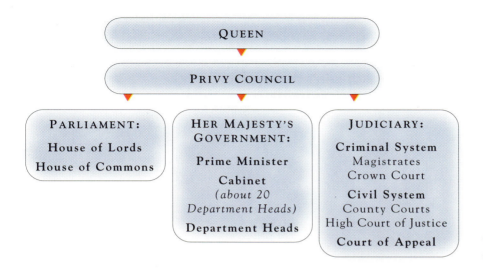

Chart of the national government

Moving Power to Parliament

In many countries, the monarch had absolute power—the power to do whatever he or she wanted. This is not so in the United Kingdom. The power of the monarch has long been limited by Parliament. England's Parliament has been meeting for more than 700 years. For that reason, it is sometimes called the "Mother of Parliaments." Most of the democracies of the world have a legislative system based on the English Parliament. The name *Parliament* is based on a Latin word for "discussion."

Under Henry II, the king's council of advisors turned into a more organized system of representatives from the "three estates"—the church, barons (the aristocracy), and

The chamber of the House of Lords

boroughs (towns). When Henry III disagreed with his council, he tried to dismiss it, but Simon de Montfort, Henry's brother-in-law, led a rebellion against the king. After Simon won a major battle in 1264, a meeting of representatives from the entire nation was called for the first time. Also for the first time, the council included common people from the middle class. This is the event celebrated as Parliament's anniversary.

Probably late in the thirteenth century, the representatives from the towns (the boroughs) and country (the shires) began to meet separately from the aristocrats who made up the House of Lords. The new group became the House of Commons.

The House of Lords consists of two groups of people referred to as the Lords Spiritual and the Lords Temporal. The Lords Spiritual are the two archbishops (Canterbury and York), as well as the twenty-four bishops of the Church of England. The Lords Temporal are the hereditary peers of the realm—the knights, barons, earls, and most other titled people.

Traditionally, the Lords were only the people who had inherited their titles (adults only—minors cannot serve in the House of Lords). But in recent years, *life peerages* have been created. Fewer than one-third of the people eligible to sit in the House of Lords participate. In 1970, Shakespearean actor Laurence Olivier, who had already been knighted,

Lady Astor and the House of Commons

Nancy Langhorne was an American from Virginia who married an Englishman, Waldorf Astor. He was a member of Parliament representing Plymouth. In 1919, he inherited the family titles and was elevated to the House of Lords. He had to give up his seat in the House of Commons. His wife ran for his seat and won. Lady Astor once said, "I am the kind of woman I would run from." But other people didn't. They kept her in the House of Commons until 1945.

Tony Blair was elected prime minister in 1997.

became the first actor ever to receive a life peerage. Sir Laurence was made a baron and took the name Lord Olivier of Brighton.

Women were not admitted to the House of Lords until 1958. Baroness Swanborough, the dowager marchioness of Reading, was the first peeress seated. ("Dowager" means that her husband had died and her son had taken the title.) She had founded the Women's Royal Voluntary Service in 1938.

Today, there are 659 members of Parliament in the House of Commons, with 529 of them from England. The head of the political party that wins the most seats becomes the prime minister of the United Kingdom. There are currently two main political parties—the Conservatives and Labour. Tony Blair, of the Labour Party, won the seat of prime minister in 1997. Since 1732, the official residence and office of the prime minister has been at 10 Downing Street on the River Thames in London. The prime minister must appear in Parliament regularly to answer questions. These sessions can become quite noisy because politeness is not expected.

Elections have to be held at least every five years, but they are usually more frequent. A new election must be held if the prime minister loses an important "vote of confidence," which says he or she can no longer hold the position. Unlike the United States, where a presidential election campaign can last a year or more, British elections usually take place within six weeks of being announced. The party that wins the election forms "Her Majesty's Government."

The prime minister lives and works at 10 Downing Street.

Margaret Thatcher, First Woman Prime Minister

Margaret Roberts was born in Grantham, Lincolnshire, in 1925. She went to Oxford University on a scholarship to study chemistry. While there, she joined the Conservative Party because she believed that the government should not be involved in people's lives. After leaving Oxford, she worked as a researcher in plastics and soon married Denis Thatcher, a businessman. She then studied to become a lawyer and became more active in Conservative politics.

In 1959, Margaret Thatcher was elected to Parliament from Finchley, in North London. Working her way up through various party positions, she was elected to head the party in 1975. When the Conservatives won the election of 1979, she, as head of the party, became prime minister. She remained prime minister until 1990, when she resigned in a power struggle from which John Major emerged victorious. Margaret Thatcher was given a life peerage in 1992 and took the name Baroness Thatcher of Kesteven.

Women over thirty were granted the right to vote in 1918.

Before 1832, only landowners could vote. That year, the Great Reform Bill was passed, increasing the number of voters. Women over thirty received the right to vote in 1918. Ten years later, the voting age was reduced to twenty-one. Today, any citizen eighteen years or older can vote.

Parliament meets in the Palace of Westminster, located on the north side of the Thames in London. The palace had been a royal residence until the sixteenth century. Parliament met there from that time until the building burned down in 1834. After that, a new, very ornate building with more than 1,000 rooms was again given the name Palace of Westminster. The

House of Commons wing was destroyed by bombs in World War II, though the House of Lords was not damaged. Commons was reconstructed by 1951 from the original plans. The famous clock called Big Ben (actually, that's the name of its bell) is on a tower of the Palace of Westminster.

Beyond Parliament

Like most governments, England has three parts to its government: Parliament, "Her Majesty's Government," and the judiciary. All three branches are officially under the queen. A name sometimes used for the government as a whole is "Whitehall," the name of the street where most of its offices are located.

"Her Majesty's Government" is the executive branch, made up of the ministers, or department heads, who are named by the prime minister. Ministers must be members of the House of Commons. Most ministers are members of the Cabinet, the group that works most closely with the prime minister. Ministers are also members of the Privy Council, which is the council of advisors to the monarch. Other prominent people are also appointed to the Privy Council for life.

The third branch of the government is the judiciary, or justice system. It is under the control of the lord chancellor, a member of the House of Lords. England, Scotland, Wales, and Northern Ireland all have separate legal systems. In England, the Crown Court hears very serious cases, such as murder and treason. Juries hear all cases before the Crown Court. Less serious cases are heard by magistrates without juries. A case

Scotland Yard in the 1700s

heard by a magistrate can be appealed to the Crown Court. A Crown Court case can be appealed to the Court of Appeal. The final Court of Appeal is the House of Lords, but only if the case involves an important principle of law.

England has forty-three separate police forces. The minister called the home secretary oversees the police forces, each of which is managed by a chief constable. The police force popularly called Scotland Yard is actually the Metropolitan Police of London. The name comes from the location of the original building, where important visitors from Scotland stayed centuries ago. The name stuck, even when the police moved in 1890 to the red-brick building on the Thames made famous in movies, and then into a modern building in the 1960s. Scotland Yard can be called in by any of the other police forces if they need help to solve a case.

London, the Capital

Samuel Johnson, an eighteenth-century writer and creator of the first modern dictionary, said, "Sir, when a man is tired of London, he is tired of life." It's very difficult to get tired of London. In 1996, an estimated 22 million visitors went to Great Britain, mostly through London.

London was founded by the Romans as Londinium. It started as a village that grew up around the first wooden bridge to span the River Thames, and the Romans eventually built a wall around it, probably to protect themselves. The wall kept the village from growing until the seventeenth century. Today, the 1-square-mile (2.6-sq-km) area within the wall is the City of London, the old financial heart of the city.

In 1666, the City of London was almost wiped out by the Great Fire, which burned for four days. Architect Sir Christopher Wren designed replacements for most of the eighty-eight churches that were destroyed in the fire, including the famous St. Paul's Cathedral.

For most of those early centuries, the only way to cross the Thames was by rowing or on the Old London Bridge (famous for "falling down" in the childhood song). Built in 1176, it had houses and shops all along its length. It lasted

The Great Fire of London destroyed the city in 1666.

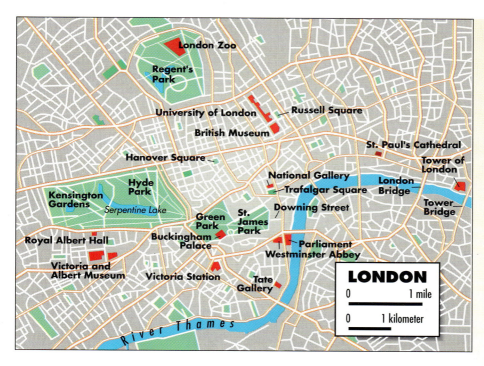

London Zoo
Regent's Park
University of London — Russell Square
British Museum
Hanover Square
St. Paul's Cathedral
Tower of London
National Gallery
London Bridge
Kensington Gardens
Hyde Park
Serpentine Lake
Trafalgar Square
Tower Bridge
Royal Albert Hall
Green Park
St. James Park
Downing Street
Buckingham Palace
Parliament
Westminster Abbey
Victoria and Albert Museum
Victoria Station
Tate Gallery
River Thames

LONDON

| 0 | 1 mile |
| 0 | 1 kilometer |

more than 650 years. Today, many bridges cross the river. Tower Bridge, by the Tower of London, is the most famous.

By 1800, London—or "the Smoke," as it has been called— was the biggest and most important city on Earth. As people made fortunes in industry, they built mansions and stores in the area now called the West End, leaving the City and the area beyond it—the East End—to deteriorate. People who could afford to moved to the suburbs, but gradually their suburbs were overtaken by the city.

Named a county in 1888, London became Greater London in the 1960s, swallowing up many surrounding suburbs and adjacent counties. Greater London is now more than 30 miles

Opposite: **The City of London and Tower Bridge**

(48 km) from east to west and almost as much from north to south. It has an area of 610 square miles (1,580 sq km).

Theaters, shops, restaurants, museums, hotels, and the government are amazingly close together in central London. But the crowding is broken up by major parks. Hyde Park and Kensington Gardens, which are attached to each other, make up the biggest green area. People can ride horses there or go rowing on a long, narrow lake called the Serpentine. Buckingham Palace is located in one part of Green Park. Regent's Park contains the famed London Zoo. Hampstead Heath is a huge natural area with lakes, woods, and moorland.

Trafalgar Square is a popular meeting place.

Many locations in London are on squares. Squares are open blocks of land, often with grass and trees, that also help to break up the crowded feel of the big city. The incredible British Museum and the University of London stand in Russell Square. Trafalgar Square, which commemorates Admiral Horatio Nelson's victory over Napoleon, is a place where everyone meets and is graced by the National Gallery. Leicester (pronounced *lester*) Square is known for its theaters. And Hanover Square is the place for fancy weddings because of the fashionable St. George's Church located there.

History and Change

For 400 years, the economy of Britain depended heavily on the docks along the River Thames in London's East End. In the twentieth century, shipping moved eastward to Tilbury, taking thousands of jobs away. London's East End deteriorated into a slum.

In 1981, a corporation set up to revive an 8.5-mile (13.6-km) area of London Docklands started one of the largest building projects in the world. The slums were torn down, and three new areas of businesses and housing are being built. A huge exhibition hall, a large university, and several whole new towns are in the works. A new city airport lets businesspeople travel quickly to Europe. Eventually, 100,000 people will work in such areas as the Isle of Dogs or Canary Wharf, and an equal number will call the Docklands home.

London is ever changing, and ever the same.

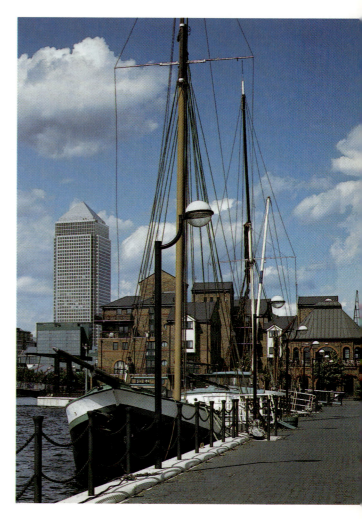

Canary Wharf in the improved Docklands area

The Business of Business

Britain was the world's first industrialized nation—one that turned from primarily agriculture to primarily manufacturing. In fact, it led the Industrial Revolution. From about 1760 to 1830, society and the economy changed greatly, leading to similar changes all over the world. The changes started when Abraham Darby of Coalbrookdale in Shropshire discovered that he could make large quantities of a hard, tough metal by smelting iron with *coke*—coal that has been roasted without air.

THEN JAMES WATT OF SCOTLAND PERFECTED THE STEAM engine, and suddenly factories became practical. Before that, textiles and most other products had been made by hand in small businesses. With the steam engine, big factories could be built to turn out large quantities of goods.

As a result of the Industrial Revolution, English society changed a great deal. Most of the working-class people who had labored on farms now crowded into cities to work in factories. Birmingham, Manchester, and Liverpool began to grow, competing with London as business centers. A new phenomenon arose—the slum. As people crowded into the cities, they lived in progressively worse squalor and dreadful poverty.

Factory smokestacks became a part of the skyline during the Industrial Revolution.

Long before the Industrial Revolution, England's prosperity depended on the gentleness of its climate. Farmers could count on their crops growing, and there was plenty of land for grazing livestock. This accounts for the fact that the most important English product for several centuries was wool from English sheep. Today, English wool is still important, but only 2 percent of the workforce is involved in the activities of agriculture, forestry, and fishing.

Wool from sheep has always been an important English product.

The main English livestock weren't only sheep. Some of the world's best cattle evolved from British breeds. Among those seen in the United States, the popular red-and-white beef-cattle breeds are Herefords and shorthorns. The brown Jersey and Guernsey dairy cattle are named for the two Channel Islands where they were bred.

England's main crop is grass. The major crops harvested are wheat, barley, potatoes, sugar beets, and a plant called rape, which produces a vegetable oil sold as canola oil.

The English are big fish eaters. Sole and plaice are both flatfish caught in the English Channel. The main catches around the other shores include mackerel, herring, and cod. There has long been a major fishing fleet working out of British ports. By agreement with the European Union, however, the British fishing fleet must be reduced in coming years because the fish breeding grounds are shrinking.

A Nation of Shopkeepers

For many centuries, people in the countryside or small villages went to larger towns to buy and sell goods. These market towns had open areas—market squares—where stalls were set up once or twice a week.

England was once called "a nation of shopkeepers." The main street (called "the high street" even if it wasn't named "High") in every town and city

has small shops that sell such items as candy, newspapers, ice cream bars or "ice lollies," tobacco, hats, small grocery items, meats, bread, and milk.

Many high streets today have a department store called Marks & Spencer. Marks & Spencer began the trend of selling quality items at discount prices. The biggest Marks & Spencer is no longer on Oxford Street in London but in a modern shopping center outside Newcastle.

One of the most famous stores in the world is Harrod's of London. It was started as a grocery store in 1849. Today, it is a huge department store that sells luxurious items from all over the world.

During the 1980s and 1990s, shopping in England came to resemble American shopping more. Today, many people buy their groceries in supermarkets. Malls, or shopping centers, are now found on the outskirts of towns. As in the United States, such centers have sometimes hurt business in the high streets.

In 1999, Europe's largest shopping center and recreation complex will open near Dartford in Kent. Called Bluewater, its parklike setting, including a large lake, will cover 240 acres (97 ha) in a former chalk quarry. More than a million trees and shrubs have been planted to turn the old quarry green.

Getting Around

England has a system of canals built in the 1700s and 1800s, just before the invention of the steam train. Originally intended for freight, the canals are now used for recre-

A Great Way to Shop

Some towns still have markets where carts, or barrows, are set up. One of the most famous streets in London is Petticoat Lane. But it doesn't even exist. The name is a 200-year-old slang term for Middlesex Street in London's East End, the centuries-old site of a second-hand clothing market. Today, Petticoat Lane sells anything that a dealer, or "pitchman," wants to sell. Equally famous is a similar market in the West End called Portobello Road (right). A song about Portobello Road is sung in Walt Disney's film *Bedknobs and Broomsticks*.

Double-decker buses are a common sight around London.

ational boating and leisurely cruises on barges. After 1905, nothing was added to the 2,000-mile (3,200-km) waterway system until a new section near Leeds opened in 1995. These canals are the only major transportation system that does not focus on London. Most other means of travel begin and end in London.

The London bus system uses world-famous double-decker red buses to go to many parts of the city. One end of the bus is open, so that passengers can hop on or off in slowly moving traffic. They pay according to the distance they travel. Single-decker green buses serve districts outside London. Every major city in England has a regional bus system.

The London Underground is the oldest subway system in the world. Also called the "Tube," it runs on 245 miles (392 km) of track through and around London. Of that distance, 106 miles (170 km) of track are actually underground—often very deep underground. Some Tube stations have the longest escalators in the world to carry people back up to street level.

Originally, the Underground was built to go between the big railroad stations that are situated around London. Richard Trevithick, a Cornish miner, invented the steam engine that ran on rails in 1801. In 1825, George Stephenson built the world's first public railroad. The Stockton and Darlington

Railway ran a distance of 20 miles (32 km) in Northumbria. The different rail lines of Britain were nationalized (taken over by the government) in 1948 and combined as British Rail. In the 1990s, however, British Rail is being transferred back into private ownership.

For centuries, the only way to cross the English Channel to France was by boat. Since World War II, people have flown across, and since 1968, a special "aircraft" called a hovercraft has carried people—and their cars—across the Channel on a cushion of air.

Many people dreamed of a tunnel that would cross to France under the sea. In the 1980s, the work of building the Channel Tunnel—often called the "Chunnel"—began as the largest engineering project in Europe. Terminals were built outside Folkestone in England and Calais in France. Railway lines now go through two separate one-way tunnels, carrying people, cars, buses, and freight. High-speed trains run between London and Paris or Brussels, Belgium. Within months of opening in 1994, the Channel Tunnel was carrying 45 percent of the freight and passenger traffic across the Channel.

London Heathrow Airport handles well over 50 million passengers every year. Gatwick, also near London, and Manchester are the second and third busiest airports in England, but their combined traffic doesn't add up to Heathrow's.

An oil rig in the North Sea

Energy

England has had a few small oil wells over the years, but the amount of oil pumped was insignificant compared to the gigantic North Sea oil field discovered off the east coast of Scotland in the 1960s. Today, more than sixty offshore wells are pumped by gigantic platforms in the sea. Most of that oil makes its way through pipelines to England, where it is broken into its components, burned as fuel, and used in manufacturing petrochemicals.

Underneath part of England lies a huge bed of coal that was mined in the eighteenth and nineteenth centuries to feed the furnaces of the Industrial Revolution. Even in the twentieth century, coal mines were places of great danger and ill health. Throughout most of the coal-mining period, entire families sometimes worked underground, including children. Between 1984 and 1994, the oil from the North Sea cut the number of working coal mines from 170 to 16.

The world's first commercial nuclear power plant was built in England at Calder Hall in Cumbria. It began supplying electricity to customers in 1956. Today, about 17 percent of England's electricity comes from its twelve nuclear power plants. The rest comes from coal- or gas-burning plants or from hydroelectric plants.

Mineral Resources

C	Coal	Ka	Kaolin (china clay)
F	Fluorspar	Na	Salt
Fe	Iron ore	O	Petroleum
G	Natural gas	Sn	Tin
K	Potash		Industrial area

Worldwide Industries

England has long been known for its research into medical drugs, or pharmaceuticals, because a Scotsman named Alexander Fleming, working in England, discovered penicillin, the first antibiotic. The English now own the largest pharmaceutical company in the world, Glaxo Wellcome.

England is also known worldwide for its fine porcelain, or bone china. About 1800, English manufacturers learned to make delicate but strong, almost transparent dishes and decorative

An interior view of Lloyd's of London

objects from bone ash and clay found mostly in the West Country. Spode and Royal Doulton are two big manufacturers of bone china. Josiah Wedgwood popularized Jasperware, beautiful pottery with white raised figures on a blue background. Today, the company employs more than 6,000 people.

Rolls-Royce, best known for its very special—and very expensive—cars, is also the world's third-largest manufacturer of airplane engines. Jaguar is owned by British Ford, which designed the Escort, now popular in the United States and Canada.

British Aerospace designed and built the Concorde supersonic airliner with the French. It now belongs to the group of European firms that created the Airbus, which has taken a lot of business from the Boeing Company of Seattle, Washington. This group is now developing the world's biggest airliner, an Airbus that will carry 550 people.

Lloyd's of London, a huge insurance organization, began insuring British shipping around the world hundreds of years ago. In the twentieth century, it became famous for being willing to insure such odd things as the possibility of a satellite falling on a man or the fertility of a racehorse. However, in the 1980s, Lloyd's had to pay out more than $12 billion in losses due to environmental disasters. For a while it looked as if the ancient organization would fold, but the government worked out a rescue, and Lloyd's is back business.

What the United Kingdom Grows, Makes, and Mines

Agriculture

Wheat	13,100,000 metric tons
Sugar beets	8,125,000 metric tons
Potatoes	7,065,000 metric tons

Manufacturing *(in English pounds sterling)*

Food and beverages	16,749,000,000
Electrical and optical equipment	14,912,000,000
Paper, printing, and publishing	14,293,000,000

Mining

Limestone	119,200,000 metric tons
Iron	7,920 metric tons
Tin	1,640 metric tons

Nationalizing Industry

In 1900, the trade unions (labor unions) created the Labour Party. In 1924, they won a majority in Parliament for the first time, and their leader, Ramsey MacDonald, became prime minister. The Labour Party believed that the government should run as many industries as possible, so that workers could be guaranteed their jobs and wealth could be distributed more evenly. They were also the first to support government-sponsored health programs and many other social services.

Starting after World War II, the Labour government run by Clement Attlee nationalized many major businesses in England—the businesses were taken over and run by the government. At first, the government-run industries were run more efficiently than they had been by private owners. Over the years, however, the nationalized industries became less profitable and less efficient.

At the same time as industry was nationalized, the medical services of England were also nationalized. Most doctors, instead of working for themselves or a hospital, work for the National Health Service (NHS). Many NHS doctors were born in India, came to the United Kingdom to study medicine, and then stayed. More than a million people work for the NHS, making it one of the largest employers in the world.

Along with the National Health Service, the people were given guarantees of housing and income. These guarantees turned the United Kingdom into what came to be known as a welfare state.

When Margaret Thatcher became the United Kingdom's first woman prime minister in 1979, the Conservative government began to return nationalized businesses to private ownership, a process called privatization. British Aerospace was among the first companies to go private. The telephone company, British Telecommunications (BT), has been private since 1984. BT is now one of the largest telecommunications networks in the world, and in 1997, it bought a major share of a big American telecommunications company. Since 1993, British Rail has been broken up into twenty-five different regions, and the right to operate the different regions has been sold to private businesses.

After World War II, during which the countries of Europe almost tore each other apart, a call was made for European nations to unite in ways that would benefit them all. Closed borders between countries would be opened. The nations would join in building an economic force that could compete with the United States, Japan, and other major trading countries. Gradually, over many years, the organization of nations called the Common Market evolved. In 1997, under the name European Union (EU), it had fifteen member nations, including the United Kingdom. Each nation sends representatives to a European Parliament.

England's Money

England's (and the United Kingdom's) currency is called the pound sterling, with the symbol £, from libra, a Roman unit of weight. For centuries, the pound was divided into twenty shillings, with twelve pennies, or pence, to the shilling. There were also half-penny (pronounced *hay penny*) coins and quarter-penny coins called farthings. A large five-shilling coin was called a crown. A smaller coin worth two shillings and sixpence was a half crown. An amount called a guinea represented one pound, one shilling. As long as English novels are read, these terms will be remembered.

Except for the pound, these coins no longer exist. In 1971, the old monetary system was changed to a decimal system. The pound remained the same (with an average value in recent years of about $1.60 in U.S. dollars), but it is now worth 100 new pence, abbreviated *p*.

Some of the EU Parliament's decisions don't bother the English too much. For example, the EU decided that all the countries involved should use the metric system. The changeover from the old inches, pounds, and quarts was gradual, but in late 1995, all British businesses officially made the switch to the metric system.

In other ways, England is reluctant to let itself come under the control of other nations. For example, the English don't want the EU to control immigration. They also are reluctant to join in a common currency. If it happens, the currency used by all EU nations will probably be called the Euro.

The Cost of Being Upper Class

In the upper classes, it was regarded as important that family estates not be broken up, because that's where the family wealth lay. It became the custom for the oldest son to inherit all the land. This was called *primogeniture*, meaning "first-born." By tradition, then, the first son inherited the estate and the title; a second son was supposed to go into the military, and a third into the church. A fourth son was usually out of luck, with no inheritance and no planned career.

The success of these large estates depended on farming to help pay for them. However, after World War II, farming income dropped because cheap farm labor was no longer available. Also, the Labour Parliament passed an inheritance-tax law that required the heirs to big estates to pay big taxes. A few families owned so much land that they could keep paying the taxes generation after generation. They had to find ways to keep their estates earning money to pay the taxes. Many great houses have now been opened to the public. Tourists pay a fee to walk through the historic rooms, perhaps hoping to see English ghosts. Some large houses have been turned into hotels. Others were sold for use as schools or business offices.

Some estate owners have used imaginative ways to keep their stately homes in the family. In 1970, the duke of Bedford, who owns Woburn Abbey in Bedfordshire, opened Safari Country, a drive-through park with wild animals. Woburn Abbey has been so successful at breeding endangered animals that fifty Père David's deer have been sent back to China, where they had been extinct for more than 100 years. The 400-year-old manor house at Beaulieu Abbey in Hampshire features the National Motor Museum developed by the owner, Lord Montagu. It has one of the most complete collections of historic cars in the world. Longleat House in Wiltshire, owned by the marquess of Bath, is proud of its white tiger, but it also features England's largest maze. Visitors can ramble along more than 1.5 miles (2.4 km) of puzzling trails, hoping to find their way out again.

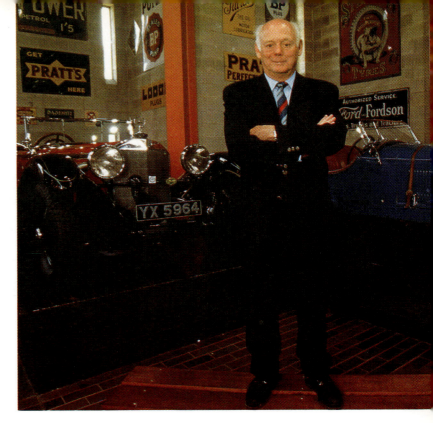

Lord Montagu, owner of the National Motor Museum in Hampshire

The English People

As far back as history records, England's people were from many lands. But from the time of the Norman Conquest in 1066 until about 1800, the people had time to solidify into a nation of people called the English.

Speaking English

THE LANGUAGE SPOKEN BY THE ANGLO-SAXONS, which is now called Old English, developed from the Germanic languages spoken by the invading tribes. Alfred the Great, king of the West Saxons, translated many works from Latin into his language. A long heroic poem called *Beowulf* was written in West Saxon about A.D. 700. Some words that survive from Old English are *write*, *oxen*, and *bring*.

Later invaders affected the language, too. Danish words and concepts are important parts of English, as are French words. English did not become the primary language of England's literature until the fourteenth century, when Geoffrey Chaucer wrote *The Canterbury Tales*. His language is called Middle English. King Henry V made English the official language. This variety of sources gives English perhaps the largest vocabulary of any language.

Early Modern English was fully in use by the time the Authorized, or "King James," Version of the Bible was created during the reign of James I. However, the spellings and meanings were not standardized into Modern English until the eighteenth century, when the first English dictionaries were published.

In recent centuries, people in the East End of London developed a kind of language called Cockney rhyming slang. The Cockneys are people born in the East End, especially "within the sound of Bow Bells," meaning as far as the bells from the church called St. Mary-le-Bow can be heard. Rhyming slang replaces a word with part of a phrase that rhymes with that word. For example, "Have a butchers at that!" means "Have a look at that!" because "butcher's hook" rhymes with "look." Or, "bread" means "money" because "money" rhymes with "bread and honey."

The English that Americans use is closer to the English written and spoken when the American colonies were founded than it is to the language of today's England. For example, *color* and *favor* were usually spelled in this way 300 years ago, but the English came to prefer the use of *colour* and *favour*.

Translating English into English

Thousands of words that are common in England have to be "translated" for Americans, including the following:

anorak = hooded winter jacket

chemist = drugstore

chips = french fries

come a cropper = end up badly

dual carriageway = divided highway

fortnight = two weeks

gaol = jail (but pronounced the same)

lift = elevator

lorry = truck

not cricket = not fair; not acceptable

pavement = sidewalk

Knighthood

Starting with William the Conqueror, the English king named a number of his favorite knights "barons" and gave them great estates. Those he trusted most received border territories that needed good defense. The barons, in turn, gave their favorite household knights some land. Each knight was expected to build a castle or fort and to protect the people who lived on his land. The barons usually rented their land to farmers, who served as "mini-barons," with all the rights the baron had.

This administrative and military system is called feudalism. The name came from *feoda*, meaning a "knight's fees." In return for land, each knight was expected to serve at the castle of his lord for forty days each year. However, the system changed quickly. The king's knights started sending the king money instead of going to work for him when he called. The king discovered that he could hire soldiers who were better at fighting than the knights were.

The Normans brought some colorful ideas about knighthood from the continent. *Heraldry* is the meaning of designs, colors, and symbols that represent families. The most common

A coat of arms on a building at Oxford University

heraldic symbol is the *coat of arms*, which was worn by a knight dressed in armor for battle. Heraldry developed during the Crusades to help the armored men identify each other. The English College of Arms, created in 1484, still helps newly created peers develop their coats of arms. *Chivalry* was the code of behavior that knights were supposed to follow. It, too, grew out of the Crusades, when a knight was expected to behave according to Christian principles.

Tournaments with bows and arrows, lances, swords, and axes, were primarily military exercises but, in the style of the times, a knight was expected to try to win in order to earn the favor of the woman he loved. Jousts, or contests between just two men, were often held as part of a tournament. If jousts were held just for fun, the weapons were usually blunted. If they were done to settle a serious dispute between knights, the weapons might be sharp.

Knights in a jousting competition

The Peerage

The aristocracy of knights changed into the aristocracy of the peerage in the thirteenth century, when the monarch turned a series of informal meetings with his barons into the House of Lords. Edward I invited between 40 and 100 landowners to attend a parliament to advise him. Those invitations were later thought to have created hereditary peerages for the men who received them. They became earls, a title the Anglo-Saxons had used. Their wives were called countesses.

Sir Winston Churchill

Edward III created a new superior rank, called duke, which today is the top rank. A duke's wife is a duchess. Edward named his son the duke of Cornwall, one of the titles held by Prince Charles, the eldest son of Queen Elizabeth II. Only five dukes belong to the royal family. Between duke and earl is the marquess (female: marchioness), a title created in 1385, and below earl is viscount (viscountess). The lowest categories are baron (baroness), the title given to the king's knights in medieval times, and baronet.

Commoners could become aristocrats. A man named John Churchill fought the French king Louis XIV so well that Queen Anne made him the duke of Marlborough. She also gave him a huge palace called Blenheim. Centuries later, a descendant of the duke of Marlborough married Jennie Jerome, an American woman. She bore him a son—Winston Spencer Churchill. Sir Winston was the very popular prime minister during World War II.

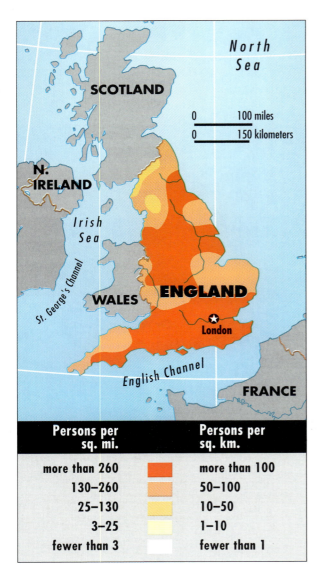

Map of England's population

Persons per sq. mi.		Persons per sq. km.
more than 260		more than 100
130–260		50–100
25–130		10–50
3–25		1–10
fewer than 3		fewer than 1

A Variety of People

Between 1800 and 1900, England's population quadrupled, with most of the growth occurring in London and other cities. This increase in urban population arose in part because work that had previously been done by individuals working in their cottages was now done by machines in big factories. Working-class women often went out to work, too, leaving their children home alone.

Today, the most densely populated metropolitan areas have more than 3,885 people per square mile (1,500 people per sq km). The only part of England with fewer than 194 people per square mile (75 people per sq km) is the area near the Scottish border, Cumbria and Northumberland.

New people have never stopped coming to England. In the early part of the 1800s, most immigrants were from Ireland. They took the lowliest jobs available, and gradually began to make homes for themselves. Later in the century, thousands of Jews came to London from Russia when the czar said they were no longer welcome there. They took jobs in tiny workshops for very low wages. The shops were often called sweatshops because the conditions were so bad.

Gradually the Jews were assimilated (absorbed) into English society. They no longer stood out as a group. In the 1940s, their place was taken by a new set of immigrants—black West Indians from the Caribbean islands and about a million people from India and Pakistan.

Concerned by how fast the population was growing, Parliament passed a law in 1968 that let an immigrant come in freely only if he or she had a parent, spouse, or child who was already a citizen. In 1976, another law was passed making it illegal to practice racial discrimination against anyone in housing, employment, or education.

Today, about 6 percent of the people in England are of an ethnic group other than white, or Caucasian. The largest non-white group is made up of people from India, Pakistan, or Bangladesh. Other groups include people from the Caribbean and China. Close to half of the nonwhite population was born in England.

The Biggest Cities	
(1995 est.)	
Greater London	6,967,500
Birmingham	1,008,400
Leeds	724,400
Sheffield	530,100
Bradford	481,700
Liverpool	474,000
Manchester	431,100
Bristol	399,200

Many people from India live in England. Here, an Indian woman teaches a class outdoors.

Popes and Parishes

Throughout the centuries, the local, or parish, church in England has been the center of much activity. Parish churches often supported schools, served as courts, and held fairs. England has more churches for its size than any other European country. Many churches are almost 1,000 years old. Unfortunately, there are fewer and fewer churchgoers to keep the wonderful old buildings in repair.

W

Hatever religion was celebrated at Stonehenge and the other stone circles of England, we know nothing of it now. It was not the religion of the druids, as many people suppose. Druids were religious and legal leaders of the Celtic people who lived in England before the Romans. In general, the Celts fled from the Romans to Ireland and Wales. By the time the Roman Empire turned Christian, its soldiers were already leaving Britain. The Germanic tribes that settled after the Romans left were pagan peoples who believed in many gods, especially in nature.

Christianity took hold in Ireland, Wales, and part of Scotland, but it was late coming to England. About A.D. 570, a Kentish king named Ethelbert married a Christian woman. Pope Gregory in Rome, hearing of the event, sent a mission to England in 597. The leader, Augustine, baptized the king and established Canterbury as the headquarters of the Christian church in England.

Christianity came to England in the late 500s.

Who Was King Arthur?

There was a real King Arthur—a Celtic leader who won twelve battles against the invading Saxons about A.D. 500. But from this bare-bones beginning, the legend of King Arthur has grown.

In the twelfth century, Geoffrey of Monmouth wrote about Arthur and his twenty-four Knights of the Round Table. Three centuries later, Sir Thomas Malory elaborated the story in *Le Morte d'Arthur* ("The Death of Arthur").

According to legend, King Arthur and his queen, Guinevere, are buried at Glastonbury Abbey near Wells. Glastonbury was supposedly founded by Joseph of Arimathea, who brought the Holy Grail, the cup used by Jesus at the Last Supper, to Glastonbury, where Arthur later sought it.

A monk known as the Venerable Bede lived in Jarrow in the old kingdom of Northumbria. He was the first important scholar of the English church. He translated Biblical writings into Anglo-Saxon. Most of what we know of the early history of England came from his book, *History of the English Church and People.*

It was the Roman Catholic Church that kept England from becoming an isolated island. Priests from the continent went to England, and English priests studied abroad. They all spoke Latin, so when the Norman Conquest occurred, there was a large body of people who could communicate with the new aristocrats, most of whom spoke Latin, in addition to French.

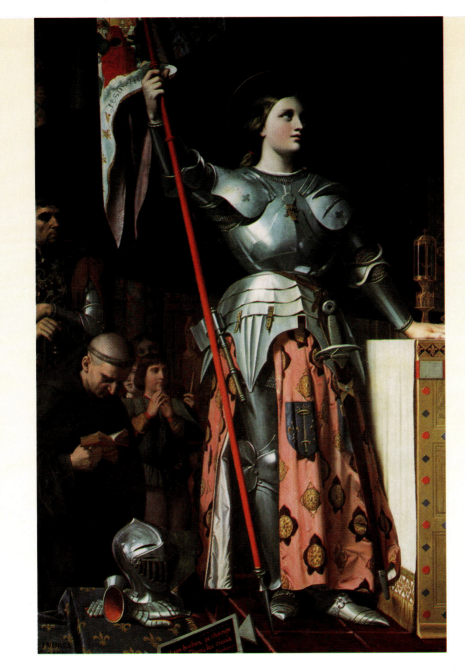

The English Make a Saint

In 1429, during the Hundred Years' War (1337–1453) between England and France, the English besieged the city of Orléans in France. The French, facing defeat, were rallied to resistance by a seventeen-year-old peasant girl who believed that God had told her to lead the army. In five battles, she proved to be a military genius and succeeded in besting the English. The young French king had not yet been crowned because he could not reach Reims, where French kings had to be crowned. The girl helped the king reach the Reims Cathedral and saw him crowned. The English captured the girl, Jeanne d'Arc (Joan of Arc), declared her a witch, and burned her at the stake.

Almost 500 years later, young Joan was canonized (declared a saint) by the Roman Catholic Church. Playwright George Bernard Shaw wrote a beautiful play about her called *Saint Joan*.

Henry VIII

Reforming England's Church

Starting about 1500, Christians in various parts of Europe were beginning to disagree with the Roman Catholic Church. They wanted everyone to be able to read the Bible, which the church had not allowed to be translated into common languages. They also wanted the church to correct some abuses of power. In the long run, these protesting groups broke with Rome and formed new Protestant churches. The Protestant Reformation occurred in England, too, but the reasons behind it were quite different. It occurred because King Henry VIII wanted to divorce his wife, and the pope, head of the Roman Catholic Church, would not let him.

Henry's wife, Catherine of Aragon (who had been his brother's widow), produced only one child who lived to grow up, a daughter named Mary. Henry, desperate for a son, asked Pope Clement VII to annul his marriage. An annulment meant that the marriage had not been legal in the first place. When the pope refused, Henry announced that the pope had no authority in England, and that the archbishop of Canterbury—who had been named by Henry—was now head of the English church. The archbishop annulled Henry's marriage to Catherine, and Henry married Anne Boleyn, one of Catherine's maids of honor, and crowned her queen.

Parliament—acting at Henry's bidding—founded a new Church of England and made the king its head. Henry had the monasteries destroyed and claimed their land and wealth. Within decades, little was left of the monasteries but smashed ruins. Most of the parish churches were not destroyed. By removing the Roman Catholic items, the people turned them into Protestant churches.

Mary, Henry VIII's elder daughter, had been raised a Catholic. When she became queen, she persecuted people who had turned Protestant. She became known as "Bloody Mary." She ruled only a few years before being succeeded by Anne Boleyn's daughter, Elizabeth, who had been raised Protestant. For decades, families who remained Catholic had to keep their religious beliefs secret.

Rumblings occurred within the new Church of England very quickly. In the late 1500s and early 1600s, the Puritans—people who believed the church was still too much like the Catholic Church—wanted less ritual and more Bible reading and prayer. Some Puritans stayed in England and eventually gained control of Parliament. Another group of people who thought real reform was impossible left England in a ship called the *Mayflower* and founded a colony in Massachusetts.

Queen Mary became known as "Bloody Mary" because she executed so many Protestants.

The Official Church

The official (or "established") church is the Church of England, or Anglican. The monarch is the head of the Church of England. There are two archbishops, one at Canterbury and one at York, who are appointed by the queen. The archbishops and the twenty-four bishops sit in the House of Lords.

The church buildings themselves are not maintained by the nation. It is up to the people in the individual parishes to pay for maintaining or repairing their buildings.

Religion is a required subject, as is daily worship, in schools paid for by the state. Most schools are supported by the state.

In 1992, the governing body of the church, called the General Synod, voted to allow women to be ordained as priests. Some male priests and members are so opposed to the idea that they have left the Church of England and returned to the Roman Catholic Church.

Other Churches

After the established church became Protestant, the Roman Catholic Church had no official structure in England until 1850. Individual Catholics and their churches continued to exist during that time, but they had no official standing. The English Roman Catholic Church now has four archbishops and twenty bishops.

Protestant churches that are not Church of England are called Free Churches. The Methodist Church is the largest Free Church in England. It was founded by John Wesley while he was studying at Oxford University. He and his brother Charles started an organization called the Holy Club. The members tried to grow spiritually through discipline, which they called "method," giving them the name "Methodists." Wesley thought he was revitalizing the Church of England, but he ended up starting a new Protestant denomination.

The Baptist Church and the Congregational Church also formed in England at about the same time, as did the Society of Friends, called Quakers. Founded by George Fox about 1650, the Quakers have no ministers at all, leaving each individual to commune with God and reach his or her own decisions about ethical behavior.

An old Methodist church in Peak District National Park

An international semireligious organization called the Salvation Army was founded by William Booth in the East End of London in 1865. Booth wanted to bring God and Jesus to poor people who were outside the established churches. Today, the Salvation Army is one of the world's largest charitable organizations.

A Muslim girl studies the Koran.

Jews began to arrive in England during the Norman Conquest. Two hundred years later, however, Edward I expelled them. They began to return in the mid-1600s and gradually attained higher and higher positions in public life. London had a Jewish mayor in 1855. Three years later, Lionel de Rothschild was elected the first Jewish member of Parliament. Benjamin Disraeli became the first Jewish prime minister in 1868.

There were few followers of Islam in England until recently. A large number of immigrants have arrived from Pakistan, Bangladesh, and the Arab countries. There are now almost 2 million Muslims in Britain, primarily in England. The first mosque (Islamic house of worship) in England was founded in 1890 in Woking, Surrey. There are now more than 300 mosques throughout the United Kingdom. The new Central Mosque in London is one of the main Islamic institutions outside the Arab world.

There are close to a million Indian immigrants living in England, and most of them are Hindus. They worship at many small temples and shrines. In 1995, the largest Hindu temple outside of India opened in north London.

CHAPTER NINE

Shakespeare, the Beatles, and Football Players

What do the people in this chapter title have in common? They are among England's contributions to the world's culture—along with Sherlock Holmes, Wallace and Gromit, Winnie the Pooh, Alice in Wonderland, Peter Pan, James Bond, tennis, Scrooge, Elton John, and punk rock.

STARTING IN MEDIEVAL TIMES, FAMILIES WHO COULD AFFORD to often employed a live-in minstrel—a musician who played and sang during meals in the great hall and for dancing afterward. Minstrels were especially popular at Christmas because people celebrated the entire Twelve Days of Christmas with gifts, good food, dancing, and plays until Twelfth Night on January 6. The person in charge of organizing the fun was called the Lord of Misrule.

Much of the joyful music began to disappear during the Protestant Reformation, when people began to fret that such Christmas joy was related to the Catholic Church. Music didn't disappear altogether. Most towns had churches, and most churches had bells. Families who could afford tutors had their daughters learn to play lutes or the piano. For centuries, it was more important that a girl learn to play an instrument well than it was for her to read.

Music was also important at court. Henry VIII composed simple songs called madrigals and accompanied himself on the lute. German composer George Frideric Handel lived most of his adult life in London. He wrote music for the king, as well as the great choral work called

Royal Albert Hall in London

Messiah there. In more recent years, Edward Elgar wrote *Pomp and Circumstance*—often used at graduation ceremonies—for Edward VII's coronation. World-famous Benjamin Britten composed such masterpieces as *Peter Grimes* and *War Requiem*.

Today, one of the world's largest music festivals is the series of Promenade Concerts, known as the "Proms," which are performed in London each year at the Royal Albert Hall. Many composers have received special commissions to compose music for the Proms. Since 1991, a National Music Day has been held each June. On a single day, well over 1,000 musical events are held in cities, schools, and churches throughout England. An all-summer festival of opera is held at Glyndebourne in Sussex.

Starting in the 1960s with four boys from Liverpool who called themselves the Beatles, British pop musicians have conquered the world. The Rolling Stones, Led Zeppelin, Pink Floyd, Eric Clapton, and The Who (known recently for a revival of their rock-opera *Tommy*) built on the fame. For the better part of two decades, groups from England topped the rock-and-roll charts. Elton John, long a popular

The Beatles had a major influence on popular music worldwide.

composer, won an Oscar in Hollywood for his songs for Walt Disney's film *The Lion King.* In 1997, a group of five young women called the Spice Girls made waves in international music.

England's Artists

The aristocrats of England traveled abroad a great deal and often brought back wonderful paintings. Many of these are located in great houses around the country. An amazing collection of paintings has been gathered in the National Gallery in London.

Master Hare
by Joshua Reynolds

England's own greatest painters were often portrait painters. Joshua Reynolds, for example, did beautiful pictures of children. Thomas Gainsborough is best known for his painting *The Blue Boy.* Because the English aristocrats loved their horses so much, one of the most popular painters was George Stubbs, who did memorable portraits of horses—and occasionally their owners.

John Constable made it acceptable for an artist to be interested in the countryside instead of aristocratic faces. J. M. W. Turner also painted landscapes, especially in the north, but he was fascinated by what light and shadow did to scenes.

Barbara Hepworth and Henry Moore were great English sculptors of recent years. American-born Jacob Epstein lived in London most of his life and worked in bronze. The works of these three sculptors are collected all over the world.

As the number of immigrants in England has risen, so has the visibility of their art. The National Black Arts Network, supported by the Arts Council of England and various regional groups, helps support black and Asian artists.

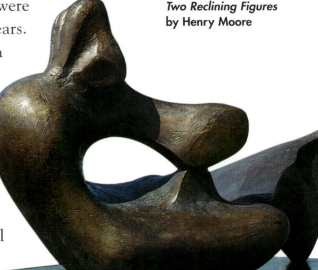

Two Reclining Figures **by Henry Moore**

Pen to Paper

Beowulf was written about A.D. 700, and Chaucer's *The Canterbury Tales* caught the fancy of medieval people. Each age has brought new writers, making English literature among the most diverse in the world.

Samuel Richardson, an eighteenth-century publisher, is regarded as one of the first novelists. His books *Pamela* and *Clarissa* were the first to tell long, connected fictional stories that revealed the feelings and actions of the characters. His idea for a new form of literature enabled people to entertain themselves by reading instead of having to listen to a storyteller.

The idea of novels caught on very quickly. Perhaps the best-known English novelist was Charles Dickens. In *Oliver*

Jane Austen is considered one of the greatest novelists in English history.

Sir Arthur Conan Doyle created the famous detective Sherlock Holmes.

Twist, A Christmas Carol, Great Expectations, and others, Dickens created memorable characters that often resemble people we all know. Among the English women who became important novelists are Jane Austen (*Pride and Prejudice*); George Eliot (*Middlemarch* and *Mill on the Floss*), who kept her real name, Mary Ann Evans, a secret; and the Brontë sisters (*Wuthering Heights* and *Jane Eyre*).

Sir Arthur Conan Doyle created the most famous detective, Sherlock Holmes. Women writers also have been particularly important in the field of mystery novels. Agatha Christie and Dorothy Sayers, for example, made the 1930s and 1940s the golden age of mystery novels. The adventurous spy James Bond, or 007, was created by Ian Fleming in 1953. Another English writer, John Gardner, has been writing James Bond stories since Fleming's death.

H. G. Wells was one of the founders of science fiction. Born in 1866 in Kent, he used his science training to write *The Time Machine, The Invisible Man*, and *The War of the Worlds*. He also helped make some of the first movies.

An English poet is regularly appointed to the position of *poet laureate*, which means "honored" or "worth a laurel wreath." The poet laureate is a member of the royal household, and often writes poems commemorating special occasions. The current poet laureate is Ted Hughes. William Wordsworth and John Masefield have been poet laureates as well.

All the World's a Stage

In the past, professional actors often wandered through the countryside like minstrels before them, putting on plays wherever they could. In 1575, an actor named James Burbage stopped wandering and built a theater in London. Twenty years later, Burbage's followers tore down the theater, moved it to a new location, and renamed it the Globe Theatre. The Globe became the theater where plays by perhaps the greatest playwright of all time—William Shakespeare—were first performed. Shakespeare was a poet as well as a playwright. In his plays, women's parts were always played by young boys. Shakespeare, who probably also acted, wrote comedies (*As You Like It, A Midsummer Night's Dream*), tragedies (*Hamlet, Romeo and Juliet*), and histories about English kings (*Henry V, Richard III*). For 500 years for people all over the world, Shakespeare's plays have remained fresh. The Royal Shakespeare Company performs in London and also in Stratford-on-Avon, Shakespeare's birthplace, where a major festival is held every summer.

London is still a center of world drama, with about 100 theaters for live productions in active use. Irish playwright George Bernard Shaw wrote a number of thoughtful and

The Globe Spins Again

The remains of the original Globe Theatre, which burned down, were excavated by archaeologists in 1989. At a nearby site, a reproduction of the Globe was built (above). It opened in 1996. Because no plans for the original theater existed, it was designed by agreement of many Shakespeare and Elizabethan experts. There are no nails in the building, only wooden pegs to hold boards together. The audience sits all around the stage, which is open to the sky. The main difference between the old Globe (left) and the new is the addition of toilet facilities and lights.

funny plays when he lived in London, including *Pygmalion*, which became the musical *My Fair Lady*. Oscar Wilde's *The Importance of Being Earnest* is still funny today. Tom Stoppard's weird and wonderful plays show that theater is still just as lively going into the twenty-first century as it was in William Shakespeare's day. Andrew Lloyd Webber's musicals, such as *Cats*, *Phantom of the Opera*, *Evita*, and *Sunset Boulevard*, are popular worldwide.

Movietime

Motion pictures were being shown in England before 1900, and soon feature films were being produced. In the early 1930s, three Hungarian brothers named Korda went to London and started a major revolution in motion pictures. They hit the big time with

The movie set of Remains of the Day

The Private Life of Henry VIII. When hit followed hit, the Kordas' company, London Films, built a whole new complex of sound stages just for making movies in Denham, Buckinghamshire. Over the coming years, the British film industry produced numerous costume dramas as well as comedies and mysteries. Alfred Hitchcock made his name in British films before moving to Hollywood.

J. Arthur Rank built major studios at Pinewood, not far from Denham. Today, the Rank Organization owns a large part of Universal Studios and its theme parks in the United States. Time Warner, the huge American information and entertainment company, is building a theme park and studio at Hillingdon in West London.

A Sporting Chance

Many of the major sports played today developed in England, such as soccer (football), tennis, rugby, badminton, and cricket. In private (called public) schools, young men were expected to become hardy and to develop good character and a sense of fair play by participating in organized games, even in lousy weather. Today, enthusiasm for participating in sports has been transferred to spectator sports.

Horseback riding has a long tradition in England.

Hunting with hounds started in Saxon times, when wild cats, and even wolves, were hunted. Foxes did not become the target of organized hunting until the late seventeenth century. Over the next decades, foxhunting became a sport of the wealthy, with rigid rules and fashions.

Until the sixteenth century, a knight's horse had to be big enough to carry the man and his heavy armor. After firearms were invented, smaller horses could be bred. Arabian and other horses were imported to improve the breeds for racing. English Thoroughbreds are important racehorses worldwide.

Queen Anne founded the Ascot Races in 1711. She wanted to have a course nearby when she stayed at Windsor Castle. Ascot became the track of the aristocrats. The St. Leger Stakes race was started in 1776 and the Derby in 1779.

Flat racing—around a regular track—is controlled by the Jockey Club, which was founded about 1755. Steeplechase, which came from Ireland, was brought to England about 1790. The horse must jump over hurdles of various kinds. Steeplechase is controlled by the National Hunt Club.

The Cricket Wicket

Although cricket is played with a bat and ball, it bears little resemblance to baseball. Two frames, or *wickets*, of three sticks are set up so that smaller sticks, called *bails*, can be knocked

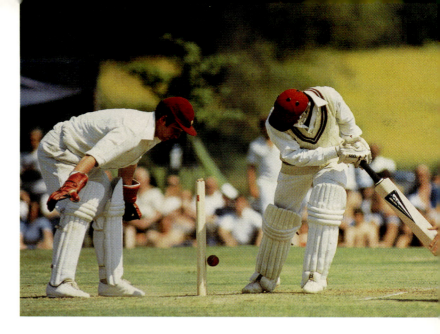

down from them by a well-pitched ball. A batsman from one team stands in front of his wicket and tries to keep the pitched ("bowled") ball away from the wicket. While the fielders are chasing the ball, the batsman runs back and forth between the two wickets as many times as he can. The period of time at which an eleven-member team is at bat is called an innings (yes, it has an *s*), and a match may last several days.

A cricket match

Cricket is at least 700 years old, but it was not organized officially until about 1788 by the Marylebone Cricket Club, which is headquartered at the most important cricket stadium, Lord's Cricket Ground in London. Today, it is played mainly in countries that were once English colonies. Test matches are matches between different countries. Women also play international test matches.

English football

Football—The English Passion

Football—or soccer—was long regarded as a lower-class sport because people could play it in the streets. One man who did not like the game described it as "nothyng but beastely fury and extreme violence."

When Thomas Arnold was head of the private school called Rugby, he turned sports into a middle- and upper-class passion.

Rugby Union Football

He believed that organized sports molded character. Rugby School revived football and gave it rules. In 1863, the Football Association was formed. Association football was primarily an amateur or semiprofessional activity until after World War II.

The European Cup is awarded each year to the best European team. The World Cup has had teams from all over the world competing every four years since 1930. England won it in 1966.

Rugby School invented another form of football in which the oval-shaped ball could be carried as well as kicked. Called Rugby Union Football, it is rather like American football but with fifteen players to a team. A variety called Rugby League Football was started in 1895 and is played mostly in northern England. It has only thirteen men to a team and favors running and passing. It became the first professional spectator sport in Britain.

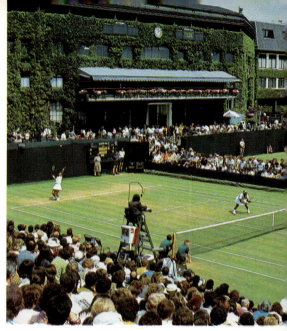

Tennis matches have been played at Wimbledon every year since 1877.

The Big Events

Tennis moved outdoors to lawns about 1870. The first lawn-tennis championships were held by the All-England Club at Wimbledon, outside London, in 1877 and have been held annually ever since. The games at Wimbledon are among the most important tennis matches in the world.

Badminton was played first at Badminton House in the 1800s. National championships are held in Birmingham.

The Henley Royal Regatta is a four-day series of rowing races held annually since 1839. The primary event is the Grand Challenge Cup, which brings eight-man crews from around the world to compete on the River Thames.

England has five major national sports centers. Crystal Palace Stadium near Croydon is primarily for athletic events, though it also has an artificial ski hill. Bisham Abbey in Berkshire emphasizes team sports, and it is also the National Tennis Training Centre. Lilleshall National Sports Centre in Shropshire has excellent gymnastics facilities and serves as the base for the Football Association's training school. The National Water Sports Centre at Holme Pierrepont in Nottinghamshire can handle everything to do with water from fishing to 2,000-meter sailing regattas. The National Cycling Centre in Manchester opened in 1994. Its velodrome—or cycle racetrack—was the site of cycling's 1996 World Cup. A new national stadium will be built in Manchester for the Commonwealth Games of 2002.

The Ingredients of Daily Life

English life is very much like life in the United States or Canada. With television easily introducing each country to others, many aspects of life are becoming very much the same. What is different is the setting of great history and tradition that has soaked into the whole of English life.

Teatime may include many delicious English treats.

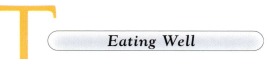

Eating Well

Today, food from probably every country on Earth can be found in restaurants in and around London and even in the smaller cities. Long before McDonalds and Burger King became widespread, however, the English bought quick meals at traditional fish-and-chips shops. This meal consists of french fries with deep-fried fish, usually cod.

Meals of various sorts and sizes were long a feature of upper-class life. A day might include five different meals: breakfast, tea or coffee at eleven, lunch, afternoon tea, and finally dinner late in the evening. Middle- and working-class people were likely to have fewer meals. For many people, tea gradually turned into a full supper, with the late formal dinner becoming a thing of the past.

Because breakfast was such an important meal of the day, a full breakfast of bacon or ham, eggs, many breads, perhaps a fish such as herring, and drinks came to be called an English breakfast. It was very different from a continental breakfast, which was just coffee and a croissant or roll and jam. These days, the English breakfast tends to be found only in tourist hotels.

English cooks have a reputation for boiling anything that can be boiled, but that is no longer true, if it ever was. English people have always served wonderful meals featuring lamb. They also have found many ways to make mutton, which is the meat of older sheep, tasty and tender. Cornish pasties, which are small pies with chopped up lamb, onion, and potato inside, are now popular in many parts of the world. Yorkshire pudding is not a sweet dessert but a baked dough that tastes wonderful with good roast beef. Each part of the country has its own special dishes.

Houses

Far into medieval times, the houses of the wealthy were usually built with defense in mind rather than comfort. A wall surrounded the compound, with a gatehouse that was fortified for keeping enemies out. Most activity of the family and its servants was carried out in one large room called the hall. Farmers lived in cottages that haven't changed in design for hundreds of years. The kinds of houses we know today were not built until Tudor times.

The number of English people who have been able to purchase their own homes has risen dramatically in recent years.

In recent years, the number of people in England who own their own homes has risen dramatically. As part of the welfare state, town councils rented apartments or small houses cheaply to those who could not afford better. In the 1980s, the councils enabled the same people to purchase their homes. In addition, many new houses are being built. In 1950, only 4.1 million homes were occupied by their owners. By 1996, that number had risen to 16 million.

Education

Education was a function of the church until the Reformation, when so many monasteries and convents were closed. Then, in the time of Elizabeth I, numerous village schools were opened, and girls went to school with boys. Only in the eighteenth century did the idea somehow get started that a woman, to be truly "womanly," should not be scholarly.

For generations, those families who could afford the fees sent their sons away to private school, called public or independent school, from the age of seven or eight. Probably the oldest independent school is Winchester College, founded in 1382. Only about 7 percent of all children attend private schools today.

Girls of wealthy families, on the other hand, were generally kept at home but separated from the rest of the household under the care of a live-in governess. They might later be sent to the continent to a finishing school, where the final "polish" was put on them before they "came out" (or made their debut by bowing before the monarch) into the marriage market.

English schoolchildren often wear uniforms.

Teenagers conduct an experiment in their chemistry class.

Until the mid-1800s, the average working-class person might be able to read a bit but probably could not write. The 1870 Education Act made elementary education compulsory, and children between the ages of five and ten had to attend school. By 1918, the age at which a child could leave school had risen to fourteen, and then to sixteen by 1972. Starting in 1944, a special test was given to all children at the age of eleven to decide whether a child should go to a grammar school (leading to college) or a secondary school, which was meant to be the end of education. Over the years, many people objected to a child's future being decided at such an early age. During the 1970s, most schools were changed to comprehensive schools, which mixed students of all abilities.

Students who leave school at sixteen take tests in several different subjects to earn the GCSE, General Certificate of Secondary Education. Students who go on after the GCSE are in the sixth form. At the end of two more years, they take tests called A-levels. Passing these tests qualifies them to go on to universities or to high-level technical training. About 67 percent of all young people continue in school after the legal leaving age of sixteen.

Colleges at the city of Oxford existed earlier, but Oxford University was officially started in 1214, making it the oldest university in Great Britain and one of the oldest in the world. Cambridge University began with one college, called Peterhouse, in 1284. These universities grew, but no additional universities were founded in England until the nineteenth century. London University was started in 1828 for students who wanted to avoid the religion that Oxford and Cambridge emphasized.

Since then, a number of colleges and universities have been founded. The universities founded by various cities outside the London area are often called "redbrick" universities to set them apart from the stone of Oxford and Cambridge. Women were allowed to attend the universities starting in the mid-1800s, but Oxford did not grant them full degrees until 1920 and Cambridge waited until 1948.

The Open University is a higher-education system that grants degrees to students who don't go to a campus to live and study. They take their courses over television, by mail, or through a computer Internet hookup. Open University classes started in 1970 and are now open to anyone in the European Union.

Oxford University is one of the oldest universities in the world.

Communications

English people have been able to mail letters since the British Postal Service (also known as the Royal Mail) was founded in 1635. It was the first postal service in the world to issue postage stamps. The neighborhood mailbox—called a "pillar box" by the English—was also invented in England.

More daily newspapers per person are sold in Britain than in any other country. The oldest weekly newspaper is probably

Berrow's Worcester Journal, which began publishing in 1690. The prestigious London *Times* began publishing daily in 1785. Probably the biggest-selling newspaper in the world is the *News of the World*. Altogether, more than 9,000 newspapers and magazines are published in the United Kingdom.

Radio broadcasting began in England in 1922. Because so many different radio manufacturers wanted permission to broadcast, the government persuaded them to form one broadcasting company that would be supported by the listeners having to buy an annual license. The British Broadcasting Corporation, or BBC, was formed. Because the licensing fee paid for the production of programs, there were no commercials. Many years later, independently owned commercial stations began.

The BBC started broadcasting television in 1936. Commercial TV began in 1955. Since 1997, there have been three commercial services supported by advertising. The average English person watches more than 25 hours each week of broadcast TV and videos.

Travel and Fun

When the Romans invaded England in A.D. 43, winding roads were already worn into the soil. The Romans built straight roads for military purposes. These straight roads are used today as major highways. The English word "highway" comes from special roads that were built up higher than the surrounding ground so that they would stay dry.

Starting in the sixteenth century, it became popular to travel to visit spas, or watering places. Some spas had an old tradition of religious miracles behind them. Others were newer and just regarded as good for the health. Bath, Wells, Tunbridge Wells, Harrogate, and Leamington were among the towns associated with such waters.

One of the main recreations for adults is going to the local pub (short for "public house"), or tavern. Even in the smallest towns, the pub is the center of news and relaxation. There are 5,300 pubs in Central London alone. Close to 400 breweries make the beer that English people enjoy.

Science and the British Museum

The British Museum was founded in 1753 when Sir Hans Sloane, a widely traveled physician and naturalist, left the items he had collected to the nation in his will. In 1847, the huge building housing the British Museum opened to the public. Among the famous things in the British Museum are the Elgin Marbles—wonderful statues from ancient Greece—and the Rosetta Stone, which was carved more than 2,000 years ago. Its discovery provided archaeologists with a way to translate ancient Egyptian hieroglyphics. When the British Museum ran out of room, another museum, the Natural History Museum, was built to house just the natural history materials. The British Museum also has a Science Museum.

With two of the oldest and best universities in the world in England, it's not surprising that England has led in scientific discovery. One of the foremost scientific organizations in the world is the Royal Society. Founded in 1660, its members include the most important British and foreign thinkers.

The British Museum in London holds many Egyptian treasures.

Opposite: **Pieces of the past, such as the remains of this church in Somerset, serve as constant reminders of England's rich and influential history.**

Looking Backward and Forward

English Heritage is the government agency that evaluates and lists properties of such importance historically or architecturally that they need to be protected. In 1995, it took care of more than 400 different properties including various castles. In addition, it has named thousands more that the owners must maintain.

The private organization that does similar work is the National Trust for Places of Historic Interest or Natural Beauty. More than 2 million members donate funds to buy and protect historic places. The National Trust also takes care of natural places. For example, it tries to buy sections of coastline that are particularly beautiful and perhaps in danger of being developed.

The Millennium Commission was established to develop and work toward plans that will improve British life in the twenty-first century. Financed by the National Lottery, it funds major projects. One of the initial proposals accepted was for the development of a 6,500-mile (10,400-km) network of bicycle trails, both in cities and in rural areas.

The Millennium Commission is also funding a huge celebration for the entire nation to be held at Greenwich, where the 0° meridian is located. As we move into the year 2000, England will start off its future with a major celebration at the point where time begins.

Timeline

c. 2500 B.C. Egyptians build the Pyramids and Sphinx in Giza.

563 B.C. Buddha is born in India.

English History

Celts begin arriving in England. 700 B.C.

Romans, under Julius Caesar, cross the English Channel. 55—54 B.C.

England becomes a Roman province. A.D. 43

Hadrian's Wall is built by Romans in northern England. c.122

St. Augustine converts the Anglo-Saxons to Christianity. 597

A.D. 313 The Roman emperor Constantine recognizes Christianity.

610 The prophet Muhammad begins preaching a new religion called Islam.

Norsemen (Vikings) take over English land. 800—880

Alfred the Great defeats the Danes. 897

1054 The Eastern (Orthodox) and Western (Roman) Churches break apart.

Normans invade England in the Battle of Hastings. 1066

Thomas Becket is murdered in Canterbury Cathedral. 1170

1095 Pope Urban II proclaims the First Crusade.

English conquest of Ireland begins. 1171

King John signs the *Magna Carta*. 1215

Hundred Years' War is fought between England and France. 1337—1453

1300s The Renaissance begins in Italy.

1347 The Black Death sweeps through Europe.

The Great Plague kills 1.5 million of England's 4 million people. 1349—50

1453 Ottoman Turks capture Constantinople, conquering the Byzantine Empire.

1492 Columbus arrives in North America.

1500s The Reformation leads to the birth of Protestantism.

Wales is annexed by order of Parliament. 1536

Henry VIII breaks with the Roman Catholic Church and names himself head of the Church of England. 1542

English History

Sir Walter Raleigh attempts to found Virginia.	**1584**
Spanish Armada is destroyed by English ships.	**1588**
Great Fire of London destroys four-fifths of the city.	**1666**
Industrial Revolution begins in England.	**c.1760**
Britain loses American colonies.	**1775–83**
British and Irish Parliaments are joined.	**1801**
Wellington conquers Napoleon's forces.	**1815**
Labour Party is created.	**1900**
The Irish Free State (now the Republic of Ireland) wins independence from the United Kingdom.	**1921**
India becomes independent of British rule.	**1947**
National Health Service begins.	**1948**
Margaret Thatcher becomes Britain's first woman prime minister.	**1979**
Britain defeats Argentina in the Falkland's War.	**1982**
Britain hands Hong Kong over to China.	**1997**

World History

1776	The Declaration of Independence is signed.
1789	The French Revolution begins.
1865	The American Civil War ends.
1914	World War I breaks out.
1917	The Bolshevik Revolution brings Communism to Russia.
1929	Worldwide economic depression begins.
1939	World War II begins, following the German invasion of Poland.
1957	The Vietnam War starts.
1989	The Berlin Wall is torn down, as Communism crumbles in Eastern Europe.
1996	Bill Clinton is reelected U.S. president.

Fast Facts

Official name: *England* refers only to the larger part of the island of Great Britain, excluding Scotland and Wales. The official name of the country to which it belongs is *the United Kingdom of Great Britain and Northern Ireland.*

Queen Elizabeth II
and Prince Philip

Capital: London (also the capital of the United Kingdom)

Official language: English

Flag of the United Kingdom

Portobello Road

Official religion:	Church of England (Church of Scotland in Scotland; no established church in Northern Ireland or Wales)
National anthem:	"God Save the Queen" (also the anthem of the United Kingdom)
Government:	The United Kingdom is a constitutional monarchy with two legislative houses (House of Lords and House of Commons). The chief of state is the sovereign, and the head of government is the prime minister.
Area:	50,356 square miles (130,422 sq km)
Bordering countries:	England is bordered by Scotland to the north and Wales to the west.
Highest elevation:	Scafell Pike in the Lake District, 3,210 feet (978 m)
Lowest elevation:	Usually sea level, but when the tide is out near Ely in the Fen Country, a small section of exposed land is actually some feet below sea level

Average temperatures:

in January	*in July*
41°F (5°C)	62°F (16.5°C)

Average annual rainfall:

East coast	20 inches (51 cm)
Western and northern hills	40 inches (102 cm)
Lake District	130 inches (330 cm)

England's population (1995): 48,707,500 (United Kingdom: 58,395,000)

Population of largest cities in England:

Greater London	6,967,500	Sheffield	530,100
Birmingham	1,008,400	Bradford	481,700
Leeds	724,400		

Famous landmarks: ▶ *Windsor Castle, Berkshire.* The oldest royal residence still in use, founded in the time of William the Conqueror.

▶ *The Tower of London.* A castle built by William the Conqueror in 1078. Its name comes from the White Tower, which today houses the Crown Jewels of England.

▶ *Westminster Abbey, London.* The burial place of sixteen English monarchs as well as many of England's famous authors.

▶ *Stonehenge.* A prehistoric open-air sanctuary, located about 8 miles (13 km) north of Salisbury.

▶ *The city of Bath.* The location of extensive Roman thermal baths, about 105 miles (169 km) west of London.

▶ *Canterbury Cathedral.* Located 55 miles (88 km) southeast of London. It is the site of the shrine of Thomas Becket and the seat of the archbishop of Canterbury, the highest position below the sovereign, in the Church of England. Canterbury Cathedral was also the final destination of Chaucer's pilgrims in *The Canterbury Tales.*

Industry: England's chief crops are barley, wheat, potatoes, and sugar beets. England also has rich grazing land for cattle and sheep. The English soil supplies three-quarters of England's food needs. Nevertheless, industry and manufacturing have outpaced agriculture in terms of gross national product.

The most lucrative mineral resource of the United Kingdom is oil, located in the North Sea. In England itself, however, coal has been the most important mineral resource for the economy, helping to fuel England's Industrial Revolution. Other important mineral extracts include sand, gravel, limestone, dolomite, and clay. Gold and silver deposits are still the property of the royal family.

England has one of the most industrialized economies in the world. Major manufacturing industries include iron and steel, electronics, and textile production. The United Kingdom as a whole is also one of the world's largest exporters of automobiles and has a thriving aerospace industry.

Currency: The primary unit of English money is the pound sterling, a paper currency of 100 pence. Aside from a 1-pound note, there are notes of 5, 10, 15, 20, and 50 pounds and coins of 1, 2, 5, 10, and 50 pence, as well as coins of 1 and 2 pounds. This system came into use on February 15, 1971. Previously, the pound was divided into 20 shillings worth 12 pence each. 1997 exchange rate: U.S. $1 = £.625 (£1=U.S.$1.60)

Weights and measures: Metric system

Literacy: Virtually 100%

To Find Out More

Nonfiction

- Fisher, Leonard Everett. *The Tower of London*. New York: Macmillan, 1987.

- Hibbert, Christopher. *The Story of England*. London: Phaidon Press, 1992.

- Lace, William W. *Elizabethan England*. San Diego, CA: Lucent Books, 1995.

- ————.*The Battle of Hastings*. San Diego, CA: Lucent Books, 1996.

- ————.*The Wars of the Roses*. San Diego, CA: Lucent Books, 1996.

- Lane, Peter. *Roman Britain*. London: B. T. Batsford, 1980.

- Lerner Geography Department Staff. *England in Pictures*. Minneapolis: Lerner Publications, 1992.

- Martell, Hazel M. *The Vikings and Jorvik*. New York: Macmillan Children's Group, 1993.

- Penner, Lucille R. *Knights and Castles*. New York: Random House, 1994.

Biography

- Driemen, J. E. *Winston Churchill: An Unbreakable Spirit*. New York: Macmillan Children's Group, 1990.

- Green, Robert. *King Henry VIII*. Danbury, CT: Franklin Watts, 1997.

- ————. *Queen Elizabeth I*. Danbury, CT: Franklin Watts, 1997.

- ————. *Queen Elizabeth II*. Danbury, CT: Franklin Watts, 1997.

- Moskin, Marietta D. *Margaret Thatcher*. New York: Simon and Schuster, 1990.

Fiction

▶ Chaucer, Geoffrey. *The Canterbury Tales: A Selection*. New York: NAL-Dutton, 1988.

▶ Crossley-Holland, Kevin. *British Folk Tales: New Versions*. New York: Orchard Books, 1987.

▶ Cushman, Karen. *Catherine Called Birdy*. Boston: Houghton Mifflin, 1994.

▶ Dickens, Charles. *Oliver Twist*. New York: Dial Books for Young Readers, 1996.

▶ Doyle, Arthur Conan. *The Adventures of Sherlock Holmes*. New York: Morrow, 1992.

▶ Kipling, Rudyard. *Puck of Pook's Hill*. New York: New American Library, 1988.

Folktales

▶ Creswick, Paul. *Robin Hood*. New York: Scribner's, 1984.

▶ Green, Roger L. *King Arthur and His Knights of the Round Table*. New York: Knopf, 1993.

Websites

▶ **The British Council**
http://www.britcoun.org/usa/
The British Council, which is the United Kingdom's international agency for culture, education, and development, offers a Website full of information about Britain.

▶ **English Heritage**
http://www.english-heritage.org.uk/
Visit English Heritage, the government agency responsible for the conservation of England's historical sites and tourist attractions.

▶ **Shakespeare Bookshelf**
http://ipl.sils.umich.edu/reading/shakespeare/shakespeare.html
Take a stop by the Internet Public Library, with a complete shelf of Shakespeare's comedies, histories, tragedies, and poems.

▶ **The *Times***
http://www.the-times.co.uk/
Read the major stories from the Times, *London's popular daily newspaper.*

Organizations and Embassies

▶ **British Embassy**

3100 Massachusetts Avenue, NW
Washington, DC 20008-3600
(202) 462-1340

▶ **British-American Chamber of Commerce**

52 Vanderbilt Avenue
New York, NY 10017
(212) 661-4060

▶ **British Tourist Authority**

551 5th Avenue, Suite 701
New York, NY 10176
(212) 986-2266

▶ **Shakespeare Society of America**

1107 N. Kings Road
West Hollywood, CA 90069
(213) 654-5623

Videotapes

▶ *England.* Traveloguer Collection.

▶ *England and Your English Ancestry.* The Heritage Corp.

▶ *London, England.* Travelview International.

▶ *Royal London.* A Doug Jones Travelog, International Travel Films.

▶ *Touring England.* A Questar Home Video Presentation.

Index

Page numbers in *italics* indicate illustrations

A

aerospace industry, 82
agriculture, 74–75, *74*
 livestock, 74–75
 map, *75*
Anglo–Saxon Chronicle, 37
Anglo–Saxons, 36
animals, 30, *30*
 dormice, 31, *31*
 wild ponies, 31, *31*
art, 108–109
 Henry Moore, 109
 National Black Arts Network, 109
 National Gallery in London, 108
 Joshua Reynolds, 108
Arthur, King of England, 98, *98*
Association football, 116
Attlee, Clement (as prime minister), 83
Austen, Jane, 110, *110*

B

badminton, 117
barons. *See* knighthood
barrows (burial mounds), 34
Battle of Britain, 51
Battle of Hastings, 38
Battle of Waterloo, 49
BBC (British Broadcasting Corporation), 124
Beaker people, 34
Beatles, 107, *107*

Birmingham, 25
Blair, Tony (as prime minister), 62, *62*
Blitz of World War II, 50–51, *50*
Bluewater, 77
Boleyn, Anne, 44, 100
borders (of England), 15–16
Boxgrove Man, 33
Bristol Channel, 19
British Isles, 11
British Museum, 125, *125*
British Postal Service, 123
Broads, 18
BT (British Telecommunications), 84
Buckingham Palace, 57, 58
Burbage, James, 111
bus system, 78, *78*

C

canals (for transportation), 77–78
Carroll, Lewis, 31
Celts, 34, 97
 Druids and, 97
Channel Tunnel, 79–80, *79*
Charles I, King of England, 47
Charles, Prince of Wales, 56–57
Chaucer, Geoffrey, 89, *89*
chivalry (knighthood), 92
Christianity, 97, *97*
Church of England, 102
Churchill, Sir Winston Spencer, 93, *93*
cities
 Birmingham, 25
 green belts, 27
 Leeds, 25, *25*
 Liverpool, 25, *25*
 London, 9, 67, 68, 70
 Manchester, 25
 population of, 95
 Sheffield, 25
 slums, 73
coal, 80–81
coastline, 13, *13*, 17

Wash bay, 17
coat of arms, *91*, 92
Cockney (language), 90
Commercial TV, 124
Commonwealth of Nations, 52
communications
 British Postal Service, 123
 newspapers, 123–124
 radio broadcasts, 124
Conservative Party, 62
counties, 15, *16*
 Greater London, 69–70
Court of Appeal, 66
cricket, 114–115, *115*
Cromwell, Oliver, 47, *47*
Crown Court, 65
culture
 art, 108–109
 communications, 123
 education, 121–123, *122*
 entertainment, 124–125
 foods, 119–120
 housing, 120–121, *120*
 literature, 109–111
 motion pictures, 112–113
 music, 106–108
 sports, 113–117
 theater, 111
 travel, 124–125

D

Darby, Abraham, 72
Dartmoor National Park, 32, *32*
Diana, Princess of Wales, 56–57, *57*
Dickens, Charles, 109–110
Disraeli, Benjamin (as prime minister), 104
Docklands (London), 71, *71*
dormice, 31, *31*
Downs, 19–20
Doyle, Sir Arthur Conan, 26, 110, *110*

Drake, Francis, 45
Druids, 9, 97

E

Early Modern English (language), 90
Easter Rebellion, 49–50
economy, 71
  effect of Industrial Revolution on, 72
  family estates, 86–87
  market squares, 75–76, *76*
  money, 85, *85*
education, 121–123, *122*
  for boys, 121
  Education Act of 1870, 122
  finishing school, 121
  GCSE (General Certificate of
    Secondary Education), 122
  for girls, 121
  independent schools, 121
  Oxford University, 123, *123*
Education Act of 1870, 122
Edward I, King of England, 42
Edward III, King of England (as King
  of France), 43
Edward VI, King of England, 44
Edward VIII, King of England, 56
  abdication of, 56
elections, 63–64
  Great Reform Bill, 64, *64*
Elgar, Edward, 107
Elizabeth I, Queen of England, 45
Elizabeth II, Queen of England, 55
energy
  coal, 80–81
  nuclear power, 81
  oil, 80, *80*
English Heritage agency, 126
English Roman Catholic Church, 102
entertainment, 124–125
  British Museum, 125, *125*
  National History Museum, 125
  pubs, 125
estuaries, 17–18
EU (European Union), 52, 85–86
executive branch (of government).

See "Her Majesty's Government"

F

feudalism, 91
finishing school, 121
firth (fjord), 15
flags
  St. George's Cross, 56
  Union Jack, 56
Fleming, Alexander, 81
fogs, 26
foods, 119–120
  teatime, *119*
football, 115–116
  Association football, *115*, 116
  Rugby League Football, 116
  Rugby Union Football, 116, *116*

G

gardens, 28–30
  hedgerows, 29–30
GCSE (General Certificate of
  Secondary Education), 122
geography, 15–16
  borders (of England), 15–16
  Broads, 18
  coastline, 13, *13*
  Downs, 19–20
  estuaries, 17–18
  highlands, 16
  Ice Age and, 14
  map, *12*
  Midlands, 16
  moors, 20–21
  Scafell Pike, 22
  tors, 32, *32*
  Wash bay, 17
  wolds, 17
George I, King of England, 48
George III, King of England, 48, *48*
Germany, attack on England by,
  50–51
Glaxo Wellcome Pharmaceuticals, 81
Globe Theatre, 111–112, *112*
government
  chart of, 59

Conservative Party, 62
Court of Appeal, 66
Crown Court, 65
elections, 63
"Her Majesty's Government", 63, 65
House of Commons, 60
House of Lords, 60–61, *60–61*
judiciary branch, 65
Labour Party, 62, 83
magistrates, 65–66
prime minister, 62
Privy Council, 65
three estates, 59–60
Great Charter. *See* Magna Carta
Great Fire (in London), 67, *67*
Great Reform Bill, 64, *64*
Greater London county, 69–70
green belts, 27

H

Hadrian's Wall, 35, 53, *53*
Handel, George Frideric, 106–107
Hanover
  Kings of, 49
  Queens of, 49
Harrod's of London, 76
Harry, Prince of Wales, 57, *57*
Heathrow Airport (London), 80
hedgerows, 29–30
Henry I, King of England, 40, *40*
Henry II, King of England, 40
Henry V, King of England (English
  language and), 89
Henry VII, King of England, 42–45
Henry VIII, King of England,
  42–44, 100, *100*
  Anne Boleyn and, 44, 100
"Her Majesty's Government", 63, 65
heraldry (knighthood), 91–92
highlands (of Scotland), 16
Hinduism, 104
Hitler, Adolf, 50–51
holidays, 126
"horse on the hill" (Wiltshire), *22*
horse racing, 114

House of Commons, 60–62
   Lady Astor and, 61
House of Lords, 60–61, *60–61*
   Sir Laurence Olivier and, 61–62
   Swanborough, Dowager
   Marchioness of Reading and, 62
housing, 120–121, *120*
hovercrafts, 79
Humber River, 17
hunting, 114

I
Ice Age, effect on geography, 14
immigration, 94–95, *95*
independent schools, 121
India, independence of, 52, *52*
Industrial Revolution, 72–73, *73*
   Abraham Darby and, 72
   James Watt and, 73
industry, 83
   aerospace, 82
   automotive, 82
   Lloyd's of London, 82, *82*
   nationalizing, 83–84
   pharmaceuticals, 81
   porcelain, 81–82
   privatization of, 84
Ireland
   Irish Republic, 50
   Norman control of, 42
   Northern Ireland, 50
   revolt against England by, 49–50
Islamic religion, 104, *104*
islands, 22–23

J
James I, King of England, 47
   attitude toward Parliament, 47
James II, King of England, 47–48
James VI, King of Ireland (as King of
   England), 43
Joan of Arc (Jeanne d'Arc), 99, *99*
John, King of England, 41–42
jousts, 92, *92*
Judaism, 104

judiciary branch (of government), 65
   Court of Appeal, 66
   Crown Court, 65
   magistrates, 65–66

K
knighthood
   chivalry, 92
   coat of arms, *91*, 92
   feudalism, 91
   heraldry, 91–92
   jousts, 92, *92*
knights (barons), 38
Korda brothers,
   motion pictures and, 112–113

L
Labour Party, 62, 83
Lake District National Park, *19*
lakes, 22
Lancaster, Kings of, 42
Langhorne, Nancy (Lady Astor), 61
language
   Cockney (slang), 90
   compared to American English, 90
   Early Modern English, 90
   Middle English, 89
   Old English, 89
Leeds, 25, *25*
literature, 109
   Jane Austen, 110, *110*
   Charles Dickens, 109–110
   Sir Arthur Conan Doyle, 26, 110, *110*
   poet laureate, 110–111
   Samuel Richardson, 109
Liverpool, 25, *25*
livestock, 74–75
Lloyd's of London, 82, *82*
London, 9, 67, 68, 70
   Docklands, 71, *71*
   Great Fire, 67, *67*
   Greater London, 69–70
   Heathrow Airport, 80
   map of, 69
   parks in, 70

squares, 70–71, *70*
   theaters in, 111
   Trafalgar Square, 70, *70*
London Films, 113
London Underground (subway system), 78

M
MacDonald, Ramsey (as prime minister), 83
madrigals, 106
magistrates, 65–66
Magna Carta, 42
Manchester, 25
maps
   agricultural, *75*
   British Empire in 1939, *46*
   geographical, *12*
   London, *69*
   minerals, *81*
   population, *94*
   topographical, *18*
market squares, 75–76, *76*
Marks & Spencer department stores, 76
Mary, Queen of England, 101, *101*
Master Hare, *108*
Methodist Church, 102–103, *103*
Metropolitan Police of London, 66, *66*
Middle English (language), 89
Midlands, 16
Midsummer Day, 9
Millennium Commission, 126
mineral map, *81*
minstrels, 106
monarchy, 55–58
   taxpayer support of, 58
money, 85, *85*
Moore, Henry, 109
   Two Reclining Figures, *109*
moors, 20–21
   wild ponies on, *31*
motion pictures, 112–113, *113*
   Korda brothers, 112–113
   London Films, 113
   Rank Organization, 113

music, 106–108
    Beatles, 107, *107*
    Edward Elgar, 107
    George Frideric Handel, 106–107
    madrigals, 106
    Promenade Concerts, 107

N

Napoleonic Wars, 48
National History Museum, 125
National Motor Museum, 87, *87*
National Trust for Places of Historic
    Interest or Natural Beauty, 126
newspapers, 123–124
NHS (National Health Service), 84
Normans
    conquest of England by, 38, *38*, 98
    Kings of, 40–41
nuclear power, 81

O

oil, 80, *80*
Old English (language), 89
Old London Bridge, 67, 69
Oliver, Lord of Brighton, 62
Olivier, Sir Laurence, 61
    as Lord Oliver of Brighton, 62
Oxford University, 123, *123*

P

Palace of Westminster
    Big Ben, 65
    Parliament and, 64–65
parks, 31
    Dartmoor National Park, 32, *32*
    in London, 70
    Lake River National Park, 19
    Parks Authority, 31
Parliament, 47, *47*, 59
    House of Commons, 60
    House of Lords, 60–61, *60–61*
    Labour Party, 83
    Palace of Westminster and, 64–65
    three estates and, 59

pathways, 28, *28*
    Pennine Bridleway, 28
peerage, 93
Pennine Bridleway, 28
pharmaceuticals, 81
    Alexander Fleming and, 81
    Glaxo Wellcome, 81
Philip, Duke of Edinburgh, 55
Picts, Rome and, 35
Plantagenets, 40
    Kings of, 41
poet laureate, 110–111
pollution
    fog and, 26
    of rivers, 21
population, 94
    immigration and, 94–95, *95*
population map, *94*
porcelain manufacturing, 81–82
Portobello Road, 77, *77*
Potter, Beatrix, 30–31
pound sterling, 85, *85*
prime ministers
    Clement Attlee, 83
    Tony Blair as, 62, *62*
    Sir Winston Spencer Churchill,
      93, *93*
    Benjamin Disraeli as, 104
    Ramsey MacDonald, 83
    residence of, 62, 63
    Margaret Thatcher as, 63, *63*,
      84
    vote of confidence and, 63
primogeniture, 86–87
Prince Consort, 55
privatization (of industry), 84
Privy Council, 65
Promenade Concerts, 107
Protestant Reformation, 100–101
pubs (public houses), 125
Puritans, 101

Q

Quakerism, 103

R

radio broadcasts, 124
railroad systems, 78–79
    Channel Tunnel, 79–80, *79*
Raleigh, Sir Walter, 45
Rank Organization (motion pictures),
    113
religion, 96–97
    Christianity, 97–98, *97*
    Church of England, 102
    Druids, 97
    English Roman Catholic Church, 102
    Hinduism, 104
    Islamic, 104, *104*
    Joan of Arc (Jeanne d'Arc), 99, *99*
    Judaism, 104
    Mary, Queen of England and, 101,
      101
    Methodist Church, 102–103, *103*
    Protestant Reformation, 100–101
    Puritans, 101
    Quakerism, 103
    Salvation Army, 103
    Venerable Bede, 98
Reynolds, Joshua, 108
    Master Hare, 108
Richard III, King of England, 43
    death of, 43
Richard the Lionhearted, 41, *41*
Richardson, Samuel, 109
rivers
    Dee, 16
    estuaries, 17–18
    Humber, 17
    pollution of, 21
    Severn, 19
    Thames, 18, 21, 67
    Tweed, 15
    Wye, 16
Rome, 36
    conquest of England by, 34–35
    Picts and, 35
rowing races, 117
Royal Society, 125

Rugby League Football, 116
Rugby Union Football, 116, *116*

S
Salvation Army, 103
Scafell Pike, 22
schools, sports in, 113
science, Royal Society and, 125
Scotland, 11
    English borders of, 15
    highlands, 16
Scotland Yard. *See* Metropolitan
    Police of London
Severn River, 19
Shakespeare, William, 111
Shaw, George Bernard, 111
Sheffield, 25
shillings, 85
shopping, 77
    Bluewater, 77
    Harrod's of London, 76
    market squares, 75–76, *76*
    Marks & Spencer department
    stores, 76
soccer. *See* football
Spain, invasion of England by, 45–46
sports, 113–117
    badminton, 117
    cricket, 114–115, *115*
    football, 115–116, *115*
    horse racing, 114
    hunting, 114
    in schools, 113
    national sports centers, 117
    rowing races, 117
    tennis, 117, *117*
squares (in London), 70–71, *70*
St. George's Cross (flag), 56
St. Paul's Cathedral, 51, *51*
Stonehenge, 8–10, *10*, 34, *34*
Strait of Dover, *20*
Stuarts, Kings of, 47
Swanborough, Dowager Marchioness
    of Reading, 62

T
teatime, 119, *119*
tennis, 117, *117*
    Wimbledon, 117, *117*
Thames River, 18, 21, 67, 69
    Old London Bridge, 67, 69
Thatcher, Margaret
    as prime minister, 63, *63*, 84
theater
    Globe Theatre, 111–112,
    112
    James Burbage, 111
    George Bernard Shaw, 111
    William Shakespeare, 111
    in London, 111
three estates, 59–60
topographical map, *18*
tors, 32, *32*
Tower Bridge, 69
Tower of London, 39, *39*
Trafalgar Square, 70, *70*
transportation, 77–78
    bus system, 78, *78*
    canals, 77–78
    Channel Tunnel, 79–80, *79*
    Heathrow Airport, 80
    Hovercraft, 79
    London Underground
    (subway system), 78
    Portobello Road, 77, *77*
    railroad, 78–79
travel, 124–125
Tudor, 44
    Kings of, 43
    Queens of, 43
Two Reclining Figures, 109

U
Union Jack (flag), 56
United Kingdom, 11
United States, role in World War II,
    51
upper classes, 86–87
    primogeniture, 86–87

V
Victoria, Queen of England, 49
Vikings, occupation of England by, 37,
    37

W
Wales, 11
    English borders of, 15–16
War of 1812, 48
Wars of the Roses, 43–44, *44*
Wash bay, 17
Watt, James, 73
weather, 23–26, *24*
    fogs, 26
    rainfall, 24
    temperature variations, 23
Wellesley, Arthur, Duke of
    Wellington, 48–49
West Country, 18–19
Westminster Abbey, 55, *55*
William, Prince of Wales, 57, *57*
William the Conqueror, King of
    England, 38–40
Wiltshire ("horse on the hill"), *22*
Wimbledon, 117, *117*
Windsor Castle, 57
    partial destruction of, 58
wolds, 17
World War I, 49
World War II
    Blitz of, 50–51, *50*
    St. Paul's Cathedral and, 51, *51*
Wye River, 16

Y
York, Kings of, 42

Meet the Author

Jean F. Blashfield delights in learning lots of fascinating, though not always important, things about places and the people who live in them. She says that when writing a book for young people, she's often as challenged by what to leave *out* of the book as what to put in. This was especially true for the book on England, because so much of America's historical culture is based on British history, and because she's been to England so often that she has a memory packed with many little stories.

When she first visited England on a college choir tour, she made up her mind that she would go back. After developing the *Young People's Science Encyclopedia* for Children's Press, she kept that promise to herself and returned to London to live. She spent three years within the sound of the lions in Regent's Park, just around the corner from 221B Baker Street, where Sherlock Holmes lived.

She took every opportunity she could to travel, visiting the Lake District, Cornwall, and many places in between. She went to theaters, ballets, concerts, art galleries, and libraries, absorbing all she could of contemporary London. Somehow, she also found the time to work at two different publishing companies. While there, she wrote her first books, retelling Gilbert and Sullivan operettas for young people.

Since then, she has returned to England often (but not often enough! she says), while writing about seventy books, most of them for young people. Besides writing about interesting places, she also loves history and science. In fact, one of her advantages as a writer is that she becomes fascinated by just about every subject she investigates. She has created an encyclopedia of aviation and space, written popular books on murderers and house plants, and had a lot of fun creating a book on the things women have done, called *Hellraisers, Heroines, and Holy Women*.

She was the founder of the *Dungeons & Dragons* book department at TSR, Inc., and became avidly interested in medieval history. Nowadays she has trouble keeping the fantasy out of her medieval world, but she thinks she stuck just to the facts in this book.

Jean Blashfield was born in Madison, Wisconsin, and lived many other places. She graduated from the University of Michigan and worked for publishers in Chicago and Washington, D.C. But she returned to the Lake Geneva area in southern Wisconsin when she married Wallace Black (a publisher, writer, and pilot) and began to raise a family. She has two college-age children, three cats, and two computers in her Victorian home in Delavan. In addition to researching via her computers, she produces whole books on the computer—scanning pictures, creating layouts, and even developing the index. She has become an avid Internet surfer and is working on her own Website, but she'll never give up her trips to the library.

Photo Credits